1,000 Creative Writing Prompts:
Ideas for Blogs, Scripts, Stories and More

BRYAN COHEN

LEGAL PAGE

DEDICATION

I dedicate this book to my parents who encouraged me no matter how frivolous my pursuits seemed at the time.

CONTENTS

INTRODUCTION

My name is Bryan Cohen and I want to help you write. I'm the author of a Web site called Build Creative Writing Ideas and I'm also the author of this book.

I've found that one of the toughest things for a writer is to come up with ideas and so I've created *1,000 Creative Writing Prompts: Ideas for Blogs, Scripts, Stories and More* to help writers avoid the dreaded writer's block that I keep hearing about. These prompts have over 50 different subjects including holidays, race, romantic comedy, childhood, prom and even the American Dream.

A prompt is a jumping off point that helps you to get your brain and pen moving. Some of these prompts are questions, some are scenarios and many of them deal with your own life and memories. When you use a memory or an emotion to write from, it helps you to feel like you aren't starting from scratch. There are thousands of stories already in your brain and many of these prompts are attempts to jog your memory and to use your brain for all it's worth.

I also feel that when you use your memories and your heart for these prompts, the writing ends up coming from a place of great truth. Even if you are writing a fantastical story about a boy and his dog, if it comes from a foundation of honesty, the story will strike a chord with your readers. Successful franchises like *Harry Potter* work for a number of reasons, but I believe the main reason is that we relate to those characters. Creating from truth is the first step to successful writing.

I'm proud to say that these prompts are original and that I've put many, many hours into coming up with them. I've gotten some extremely positive feedback from users of my website and so the creation of this book was the next logical step.

I've written a few short essays to help get you started, but you can start writing from the prompts right away if you wish. So...hop to it!

How to Be a Writer

A lot of people feel like they need some kind of permission to be called a writer. Like once they've taken enough classes or once they've published something there is some tribunal that will decree that they are now in fact writers. Others feel as though they're writers even though they've never even made an effort to write more than a short story here and a poem there.

We live in a tough world full of put-downs and negative talk. If someone does not have the will or the ability to achieve his dreams he may feel the desire to kick around the aspirations of other people. We may hear this kind of unproductive negativity from our parents, friends, loved ones and those we mistakenly see as our enemies.

A writer is a person who can see through all this negativity and still feel passionate about writing. A writer wants to write and wants to figure out ways to make writing more a part of his life. There are some writers that are financially successful and others who haven't made a dime, but they are all still writers.

If you say over and over again that you aren't qualified enough to be a writer...you will fulfill your own (kind of boring) prophecy. If you tell yourself that you are a writer and you tell other people this over and over again, the opposite will be true. But how do you know if you're a writer?

If you aren't sure if you qualify as a writer, there is only one thing you need to do.

Write. Just write. Write as much as you can as often as you can. It doesn't matter if you've written anything lately, just start now. If you have an off week, month or year, it doesn't matter because you can start writing again at any time. If you have the desire to write and you can give yourself the permission to have this passion in your life then you are a writer.

This is about the time that the excuses come rolling in:

"I don't have enough time."

"Writing doesn't pay and I'm broke."

"I don't have any motivation."

Solving these problems is as easy as visiting your local library. Hundreds of books have been written about time management, financial management and creating motivation in your life. Continuing to make these excuses and ones like them, with solutions available at any time (for free, no less) is essentially laziness.

Laziness is boring. A life of spending your free time watching television and learning everything you can learn online about celebrities (or the like) is boring. If you even have an inkling of wanting to be a writer, pick up a few books that will leave your excuses in the dust and try working hard to make something of yourself.

My website, Build Creative Writing Ideas has many tips and tricks to improve your motivation and time management, so if you can't get off your butt to visit the library check it out. For those of you who are ready to write, strap yourself in and try a few of these prompts on for size. Happy writing!

How to Write from Prompts

These 1,000 creative writing prompts have been compiled from various ideas that have floated in and out of my head over the last two years. I have made as many as I can very open ended so that the same prompt could be used multiple times over.

The prompts often take the form of a scenario with a question:

"259. You see a little boy wander into the middle of a busy intersection. What do you do?"

There are multiple ways that you could choose to write from this prompt. You could launch into a first person story or explanation:

"I would immediately drop all of my belongings and run to his safety. As I run into traffic, my life would flash before my eyes and I would hope desperately that I could make it to the boy in time to save us both…"

You could make it into a third-person fiction story:

"Derrick and Joey laughed and sipped their drinks. All of a sudden, Joey noticed something out of the corner of his eye.

'What the…'

Joey trailed off as he noticed a young boy trip and fall in the middle of the road. He was all alone. Joey was the only person with enough time to act…"

Or you could transport it into another genre:

"The boy tripped and fell in the middle of the road. The truck struck him with all its force and it quickly shattered into a million pieces. The nearby cars screeched to a half and stared with their mouths agape at the uninjured boy."

What you write from these prompts could be the start of an entire story or it could just allow you to get a few paragraphs in for the day. You could write a blog post based on what you write, a short story, a poem, a teleplay, a screenplay, a stage play, a novel or anything else that requires putting pen to paper.

These are not assignments by any means. You can write as much or as little as you wish. Run with an idea until you can't think of anything else and then try another one. Write one story from a prompt and then write a completely different story from the same prompt. What you use these prompts for is up to you. If you turn one of these prompts into a million-dollar screenplay (and I hope you do) go off and enjoy yourself, because I will not expect anything from you in the slightest. I created these ideas so that writers could simply write from the heart without having to think too much so go off and make me proud :).

If you do not like a prompt, you don't have to write from it. You can also come up with a new prompt based on the prompt you don't like. Seriously, whatever you want to do with this book and these prompts, please feel free to do it. I just want you to write! If you ever have a question about where a prompt came from or what I meant by a particular prompt, feel free to contact me on my site, Build Creative Writing Ideas.

Writing Every Day

One fantastic way to use this book is to write from one prompts every day to keep yourself trained and fresh. Writing every day can be difficult to get started but once you make it a habit it'll be just like flossing (except much less gross).

The method that I like to use to integrate new habits into my life is a method developed by blogger Steve Pavlina called "The 30 Day Plan." One of the mistakes people make when trying to add a habit to their lives is that they think too far down the line wondering, "How could I possibly make this a habit for the rest of my life?"

Steve Pavlina recommends that you look a lot more short term. He likens adding a new habit to installing some software with a free 30 day trial. Try adding a new habit (like writing the prompts) to your routine for just 30 days. Choosing this time constraint allows you to easily block the month off in your calendar and it doesn't feel too overwhelming to just think about four tiny little weeks.

The best thing about "The 30 Day Plan" however is that 30 days is as long as your brain needs to make a task into a habit. You have slowly but surely trained your brain into writing a prompt every single day and now it's already a part of your life. This makes it a much simpler task to keep writing a part of your day.

Find a time of day that you almost always have free. This time should also be a part of the day that you are energized and awake. If you always get home from work tired, you may not want to choose the ten or fifteen minutes right when you return. The time should be specific and consistent. I enjoy writing in the morning after I've gone on a jog and I've had a light breakfast. Another reason I choose the morning is because if something comes up, I have the rest of the day to find time for it.

Set a clear goal for yourself. Some people set a word count per day or set it at one page per day. To start out, you may just want to require only a few sentences per day to get in the swing of things. An example of a clear writing goal is:

"I will write 200 words from a different writing prompt each day at 8 a.m. for 30 days starting August 1st."

Once your goal is set, all you have to do is start. So hop to it and let me know how it goes. Thanks so much for trying out *1,000 Creative Writing Prompts*. I wish you all the writing success in the world.

Sincerely,
Bryan Cohen
Author of *1,000 Creative Writing Prompts*
build-creative-writing-ideas.com

1 HOLIDAYS

Creative Writing Prompts: Halloween

1. Explain your most memorable Halloween: from the candy you received, the costume you wore, the environment of your neighborhood (if you trick or treated) and why it has dwarfed all of your other Halloween experiences.

2. You have a 16 year old daughter who wants to go to a Halloween party with all of her peers. You take her to the Halloween store to find an "appropriate" costume. She is resistant to most "conservative" choices. Describe the encounter, your feelings, and what you end up deciding upon.

3. In a burst of charity, you are planning to be the best Halloween house in the neighborhood by giving away the best candy. Go through the days of preparation and detail your holiday evening. How have the children reacted? Have you sample one too many of the goodies, perhaps?

4. Best Halloween costume you've ever been in. Go through the entire process of creating it and the reactions of your peers.

5. The top 5 costumes you've ever seen on Halloween. Why they were so memorable to you and why you wish you'd thought of them first.

6. You see an actual ghost on Halloween! Not necessarily an angry one, but definitely a depressed ghost. How do you help him cope with death and his haunting afterlife?

7. You are throwing the best Halloween party in town! Describe your preparation, the shin-dig itself, the aftermath, and the cleanup. Did you enjoy yourself? Did your house almost burn down?

8. Research the origins of Halloween and try to imagine what it would be like on one of the first commercial Halloweens. Write a story about a boy or girl in those early days of the holiday.

9. You and your significant other need to create a "couples" costume. What do you pick and why? How does it go over with the group? If you do not have a significant other, just use your ideal mate in the story instead :).

10. You go on a candy eating binge! Detail your feelings during the pig-out session, when you reach your breaking point, and how you feel the rest of the night (and following day).

11. You get the esteemed pleasure of explaining Halloween to a foreign exchange student. Describe the encounter and take him on his first Halloween adventure!

12. You have $5 and 30 minutes to create the best Halloween costumes possible. How do you do it and what do you go as?

Creative Writing Prompts: 4th of July

13. What is the most amazing fireworks display you've ever seen in your life on a 4th of July celebration? What shapes did you see and music did you hear in accompaniment? Who were you with and why else might it have been memorable?

14. What is a particular 4th of July celebration that really sticks out in your mind? Was there some big disaster or incredible event that occurred during one of them way back when? If not, create a story about a wacky and wild 4th of July celebration.

15. You have been invited to an Independence Day barbecue! You get there, and realize that the people there are extremely "American" Americans. There are flags everywhere, with memorabilia, army medals, etc. The Americanism is overwhelming as people keep asking you how you feel about living in the best country ever. How do you deal with such an event?

16. You have been transported back in time to July 4th, 1776. How do you insert yourself into being a part of the history of the holiday and the United States?

17. Describe a 4th of July celebration with you and several other Americans outside of the United States. Is there an Americanized bar that you can party at or is a more private affair at a hotel with copious amounts of alcohol? Go into extreme detail.

18. You are with a child who is just old enough to start asking questions about everything. How do you explain July 4th to him to ensure that he understands and doesn't ask any more questions? :)

19. What does the 4th of July mean to you as a holiday? Do you feel a strong American pull or are you just happy to get some potato salad and hang out with friends?

20. You are hosting your own gargantuan 4th of July barbecue. You have about 100 people coming over and you have 3 days to get prepared. Talk about your process from beginning to end of making it a success.

21. July 4th weekend has become synonymous with "biggest movie of the summer" weekend. What is your favorite July 4th blockbuster that has packed the seats with people and the screen with explosions?

22. You and your friends have decided to get hammered during a very American day involving a baseball game, a barbecue, and a trip to a bar. Talk about the progression from the beginning to end of this all-American day.

23. What are your experiences with other independence days in other nations? What are the equivalent holidays in some other nationalities that you are familiar with and which ones do you feel is the most appropriate celebration of a nation. Do some research if necessary.

24. Imagine that you have decided to use Independence Day to actually become independent in every way possible. What would that entail? Describe your actual "independence day."

Creative Writing Prompts: New Year's Eve

25. Talk a little bit about your best New Year's Eve kiss as the clock struck midnight. Write about the anticipation, the actual smooch, and the aftermath. Why was it so great? If you haven't had a New Year's Even kiss just write about what your ideal one would be like.

26. Write about a memorable New Year's Eve house party that you went to. Who did you know there, what did you do while you were there, and what events made it stick out? Have fun with your portrayal and really try to get the vibe of it as correct as possible.

27. What do you think your ideal New Year's Eve would be? Are you a loner who simply wants to get a feel for the world on the beach? A lover who wants to spend every last second with your significant other? A party-er? Go from top to bottom of your New Year's Eve creating your perfect way to ring in the next year.

28. Talk about one New Year's resolution that you've kept and one that you let slip by. How did you make sure that the one that worked stayed in your life and why did the other one fall away? If you had a choice (and you do) how could you get the absent one to work right now?

29. Have you ever been to one of the famous New Year's Eve sites like Times Square in New York? Talk about your experiences there if you have, and if you haven't, craft a story of your journey to a big event with a lot of people celebrating this holiday.

30. What are your top five resolutions that you would put into effect today if it was New Year's Eve? Write a story of you trying to accomplish them. Who knows, maybe you'll come up with some good ideas as a result.

31. In an attempt to drive back home for New Year's, your car has become stuck in a snow storm! You're not even exactly sure where you are, but you pull off an exit to wait it out at a diner. The snow does not stop. What happens next?

32. Have you ever opted for a non-tradition, away from the party New Year's Eve? Talk about that if you have, and if you haven't, craft a tale of an interesting event that most would consider off the beaten path for this type of celebration.

33. Create a character that is making a recap of his year on the evening of New Year's Eve while sitting at home. He is contemplating a massive change in his life and he is hoping to avoid that change by proving that his year was "good enough."

34. Despite your better judgment, you have drunk an entire bottle of champagne! And it's only ten minutes past midnight! How does the rest of your night go? If you don't remember it, write a story in which someone recounts it all to you the next day.

35. You have been handed a card by a friend of a friend at a New Year's Eve party. You open the card to find that it's from your secret admirer and that he or she desperately wants to kiss you at midnight. How do you proceed to make this a reality (or to run away from it)?

36. What are some ways that New Year's Eve is celebrated in countries throughout the world? I mean, not everyone just gets drunk on champagne and tries to smooch someone when the ball drops, right? Do a bit of research and write a story from the perspective of one of those people.

Creative Writing Prompts: Thanksgiving

37. The whole family is together and all the typical weird things that happen are in full-force this year. Detail a typical thanksgiving with your family, friends, and loved ones (and probably some hated ones in there too :)).

38. Is there a Thanksgiving that you remember as the most wonderful (or the most crazy, messed-up) holiday of your life? Write it out in full-force and feel free to embellish as much as you'd like :).

39. Your typical family thanksgiving has fallen through and you decide to spend it with your best friends in the world. Put together a story in which your best friends come from all over the world to dine at your thanksgiving table. How does it work out?

40. You are cooking your first thanksgiving dinner all by yourself! You have lots of guests coming and a whole lot of stuffing to buy. Detail the week of Thanksgiving from Monday to Thursday and talk about if you pull it off or not. What are the dishes you make?!

41. Create a thanksgiving story in which everything goes wrong (a la the movie "Pieces of April"). From the dinner to the family awkwardness, this holiday goes spinning off the axels big time. How does it all go down? Be very descriptive.

42. You are visiting four thanksgivings in one weekend (a la "Four Christmases"). How do you eat all that food? Which one is the best? Who are these people you're visiting?

43. Describe the best thanksgiving leftover creation you've ever concocted. Make one up if you've never stooped to using Thanksgiving leftovers for a month after the holiday. Whether it is a sandwich with all the ingredients or a dessert mixture with 6 different pies, make it awesome and make it tasty.

44. What is your favorite part of this holiday? The family? The food? The passing out on the couch watching football? Talk about that a bit. If you hate this holiday, you can talk about that as well.

45. Create a completely alternative thanksgiving. No turkey. No stuffing. But still tasty and interesting. See what you can come up with when trying to stick to a particular theme.

46. Even if you've never done this before, detail a touch football game with all of the members of your family involved. Grandma should be in too. Keep in mind; you've just eaten a lot, so this game will be slow-paced and hilarious.

47. You've been transported to the original thanksgiving! Pilgrims, Indians and all. Is it really as nice as we make it out to be? Did two people bring the same item? Talk about your experience in the past.

48. What are you thankful for on this gratitude-rich holiday? Create a list of at least 10 and detail how you came to be thankful of these things.

Creative Writing Prompts: Birthdays

49. What was your favorite birthday and why? Who was there? Did you have a party? What presents did you get? Be very specific about what made it so special.

50. What was your worst birthday and why? Be extremely detailed about what made it such an awful memory. As always, you can make it into a character's story and exaggerate all the details to an extreme degree.

51. Have you ever been to a birthday party that was so extravagant it actually made you somewhat jealous? If not, create a story in which a character goes to a birthday party that is completely out of his league. This especially includes the present that you got this person. Totally inadequate :).

52. How do you feel as though you will change with your upcoming birthday? Will your responsibilities change? Will your clock start ticking a little faster to do something that you've been meaning to do? Be specific and detailed.

53. Create your ideal birthday story for any age that you wish. You can re-make a birthday party or get together you've already had or plan out a new amazing celebration for the future. The important thing is to make it absolutely perfect in every possible way.

54. In a bit of magic, you get to relive each of your birthdays from the age of one all the way to now. How does it feel to be back in that high chair? What about playing party games a little bit down the road? Sitting with that middle school sweetheart you had at the time? What would you do differently and what would you make sure stayed the same?

55. Create a story in which the main character hates birthdays, and tries extremely hard to avoid telling people that today is his special day. And it happens to be the best day of his life. Elaborate to the extreme.

56. Talk about your best birthday cake experience, yours or someone else's. Did you put your face in one? Did you eat five to ten pieces of one? Have fun with this one and really flesh everything out. Mmm, frosting.

57. Write a story about throwing a birthday party for someone. Whether it is for a family member or a significant other. How did it go? Did the person enjoy him or herself?

58. What is the best present that you've ever gotten for your birthday? Not necessarily the most expensive, but the one that was the most important to you. Talk about it and try to remember where that present is today.

59. You have been given a five million dollar budget for your birthday party

(from an anonymous donor). You can only use this money if you spend every penny. What do you do with this fantastic party budget?

60. Create a story about the wildest birthday party that you have ever attended. If they have all been too tame, make up the wackiest one you can think of.

2 SEASONS

Creative Writing Prompts: Winter

61. Describe a situation in which you were the coldest you've ever been in your life during the winter.

62. It is probably difficult to remember your first snowfall as a child. Do a sort of bird's eye view account of what that experience could have been like for "little you."

63. After a big snowstorm, you and your family are trapped in the house with no place to go for at least the next 48 hours. What do you do with this time?

64. Ice skating on natural ice! Talk about a time in which you skated on real ice (not in a rink). Make up the story if you don't have one.

65. It is -10 degrees F outside. What do you wear? Detail your dressing process for the extreme cold.

66. You are building the most extreme snow display ever. Not just a snowman but an entire snow city! Talk about you and your fellow builders creating such beauty.

67. You and your dorm face off against another dorm in an epic snowball extravaganza. Detail the entire battle.

68. Driving on snow and ice takes a great deal of patience and skill. Create a story about a long ice driving trip.

69. Sitting by a roaring fireplace, sipping a hot cocoa, while bundled up in a fleece blanket. Talk about how wonderful this can be in the dead of winter.

70. What is your favorite past experience that occurred during the season of winter. Be very specific.

71. You meet the Abominable Snowman! Seems like a pretty cool dude, what do you talk about?

72. What is your favorite winter sport to watch? Talk about watching a game with your friends and family between two of your favorite teams to see play.

Creative Writing Prompts: Spring

73. It is the first warm, pleasant day of the spring season. What kind of activities do you do outside to embrace the day?

74. It is April and you know what the means: April Showers. Big time! Talk about living through a month of nearly all Spring-time rain.

75. You go on a nature walk date with your significant other. Your partner is an extreme flower lover and goes into all the details of every plant you stumble upon. What is your reaction?

76. Spring cleaning! Create a story in which you have to get rid of a lot of prized memorabilia from your past.

77. You are in a meadow that truly shows the beauty of spring. There is green everywhere punctuated by other bright colors. You close your eyes and breathe in. What is going through your mind?

78. Describe a spring gardening session. If you don't know what that would consist of, either look it up or make it up.

79. You go out of your front door and you're confronted by...bees! A spring hive of bees has formed near your front door. Write the story about you dealing with the hive.

80. You have been invited to a spring-themed potluck dinner. What spring related dish do you bring and why?

81. Time for some spring fruit picking with your family! Describe a time where your family fruit picked. This story can be made up or exaggerated if you wish.

82. Talk about your experiences with spring sports. This could be connected to Spring Training, field hockey, lacrosse. Really anything spring and sport-related.

83. You have control over the weather and can create one perfect spring day. What do you do?

84. While Spring is often a rebirth when it comes to the cycles of nature, it can also be a sort of reawakening for your own life. Many people start new habits and hobbies in the spring. Talk about some of your experiences with this or make something up that you would like to change.

Creative Writing Prompts: Fall

85. The leaves on all the trees have changed color and begun to fall all around town. How does this multi-colored landscape make you feel?

86. Despite the fact that you've been asked to rake up the leaves, you and several friends have decided to jump and play in them instead. Talk about the experience.

87. You walk through the brisk cold of an autumn morning with frost on the ground. Fall is truly in the air. What does that mean to you?

88. Pumpkins, corn husks, and scarecrows. What is the best set of fall-related decorations you've ever seen?

89. What is your favorite fall-related activity? Some examples might be a haunted hayride, soccer game, or a pumpkin patch.

90. A child asks you why the leaves change colors and fall down. How do you explain to him in a way he'll understand?

91. Where in the world would you most want to be to get the best fall experience? Write a story of one day in that location.

92. Halloween, the World Series, the annual pumpkin pie contest. What is your favorite fall event that you look forward to and why?

93. The kids have gone back to school and now you have more time with your significant other. How do you spend it?

94. What is your favorite fall related food and why?

95. You are a leaf on a tree that is undergoing foliage. What are your leafy thoughts and feelings?

96. Fall has such a distinct feel to it, that almost any story would be painted heavily by setting it in the fall. Re-write an old story and change the setting to square in the middle of the season.

Creative Writing Prompts: Summer

97. It's hot. Sticky hot. You are sitting in your house or apartment with broken air conditioning and an outside temperature of 100 degrees F. Describe your day.

98. Ring a ling! It's the glorious Pavlov dog effect of the ice cream man. Write about your ice cream man experiences.

99. The old summer job. Whether it is the snack counter at the local pool or a camp counselor at the day camp, we've all had them. Talk about yours in great detail.

100. Summer fling! Ever had one? If so, write about it; if not, make up your ideal summer relationship.

101. There are amazing family summer vacations and there are family summer vacation disasters. Pick one and have a ball with it.

102. Going to the beach or the pool to watch the pretty people walk by in their swimsuits. Detail an afternoon of lounging and people watching.

103. It is that week where all of your friends have gone out of town except for you. What do you do with your extreme free time?

104. Whether it's beach volleyball, soccer, or Frisbee, the summer can be filled with sports. What are some of your summer sport experiences?

105. The end of summer is on and the shopping for school supplies begins! How do you get the last bit of juice out of the season?

106. One of those late-night summer barbecues with a couple of cold beers and good friends. What do you talk about? Describe the evening.

107. What is your favorite summer dessert and why? Portray a very descriptive scene in which you devour your dessert.

108. You are suddenly transported to the middle of some unknown dessert during the hottest part of the summer. How do you survive and get yourself to safety?

3 MEMORIES

Creative Writing Prompts: School

109. Take a time from your life (or imagine a time) that you were bullied at school. Who was the bully and how did he or she affect you? Imagine a sit down chat with the bully in which the person could not bully you and had to share his or her feelings. What do you think you would learn?

110. What was your shining school achievement? The moment that you felt the most intelligent or the most gifted? Talk about that day, what led up to it, and how it changed your life.

111. Talk about the teacher that you liked the most in school. What made you enjoy the class that he or she taught and why was this person so memorable to the present day?

112. Talk about the teacher that you disliked the most in school. What was wrong with this person? If you had a chance to sit down with this teacher, what would you tell this person about how to change his or her teaching style (and perhaps attitude)?

113. Describe your first school crush or your first school significant other. What was it like? How did you feel walking around the school and possibly having people talk about you? Feel free to talk about the entire relationship.

114. Where were you on the school popularity scale in middle or high school (or college)? How do you think your placement on this scale came about and how did it affect your experience? Did it change the way that you are today?

115. What was your favorite after-school activity? If you were a sports player, talk about that, a band member, talk about that, a chess club member...close the door, and then talk about that ;). Describe how this activity made you feel and why it was important to you at the time.

116. Talk about a time (or make up a time) in which you were called in to the principal or dean's office. What happened? Why were you there and what was the end result?

117. Who were your best friends in Elementary school? Middle school? High school? College? Talk about what you guys and gals used to do together and why you are no longer close or why you are still close to this very day. What was your most memorable school friend moment?

118. Talk about a time that you cheated or thought about cheating on a test. If you are more moral than the rest of us ;) (4th grade geography test was the only time, I swear :)) than talk about one of your friends or peers who cheated and what the end result was.

119. You have been sent back in time (to kindergarten) and you have the ability to change your entire schooling experience. How do you change the next sixteen years of your life or so to make your life better? Does it work or do you lose some of the flavor along the way?

120. Your most awkward school experience ever. Write about it or make something up.

Creative Writing Prompts: Childhood

121. What is your most poignant childhood memory? The one that sticks out the most. Write out as much as you can remember and then fill in the details with elaborate description.

122. Who was the most important person to you during most of your childhood? Your Mom? Your Dad? Another relative? A friend? An imaginary

person? Show some examples in which you see how much influence this person (or imaginary person) had on you while you were growing up.

123. It seems like when you are a kid growing up you can't wait to get there and when you are a grown up you wish you could be back. Imagine one day in which you are granted adulthood as a child, and one day in which you are granted childhood as an adult. How do you utilize these 24 hour periods?

124. We all have that friend we had in childhood who later moved into a different popularity scale in middle or high school. Who was that friend and what was it you two enjoyed so much together when you were little?

125. What did you and your family do for entertainment when you were little? Did you play board games together? Go to movies? Go into extreme detail of a family fun night of some kind.

126. What cartoon from your childhood is the most memorable for you? What made it stick in your head so strongly? Would you see a movie of it now if were made into a big blockbuster for the nostalgia purposes?

127. How did the following things affect you during your childhood: music, books, the weather, money, love? You can combine them all into one story or do separate entries on each.

128. What action makes you the most nostalgic for your childhood? Is it seeing old pictures or going through old clothes? Something else entirely? Write a story of you going through those nostalgic actions and having various memories of your childhood.

129. How do you recall getting along with your family during your childhood? With your parents, siblings, and other relatives? Go through a typical reunion or holiday with your entire family in attendance during your childhood. Have fun going into excruciating detail :).

130. It's your birthday! Pick a party that you had during your childhood or create an ideal birthday party for yourself at any young age and write a story about it.

131. You have been given the opportunity to go backwards. You can pick an age and start over again from that age. Do you pick one or not? What age would you go to? Describe your first week with your "old person" memories in your younger body.

132. Make a list of five things that you thought were completely awesome as a child. Write as if you are that age and describe why these things were so enjoyable for you.

Creative Writing Prompts: College

133. Describe your first crush in college. If you were me, it was during freshman orientation :). It could be brief and it may have resulted from the huge influx in new people into your life, but it is an important event to recall. Describe as much of it as you can and fill in the details with creative elaboration.

134. Talk about a class and a professor that really changed your life. It may have been the professor that you went to see every week during office hours or it may have just been a lecturer that you never even interacted with. Detail why this made such an impact on you.

135. Not everybody had a freshman 15 (a weight gain of 15 pounds freshman year), but almost all freshman have a big gain of some kind (religion, friends, long walk from the dorms). Talk about the big gain you might have experienced from that first year.

136. For many people, going to college is the first time living with another person in those wonderfully cramped dorm rooms. How were your college dorm room experiences? Talk about a few big events that occurred in your dorm room life. How many times were you walked in on during make-out sessions? During...personal sessions? :) The potential awkward situations are endless :).

137. Talk about the social aspects of your college town. Was it a mostly self-contained beast (a la Penn State University) or was there an urban or country zone surrounding and influencing the campus? How did this affect your experiences?

138. My freshman year at our first big class meeting (no small feat at a state school) we had a speaker tell us to find two things in our time in college: one thing to love and one person to love. Did you find those two things? If so, talk about them, if not, talk about your close encounters.

139. Drinking. Can't help but get into that one a bit. Even if you didn't drink, what was a big experience that you had in college with drinking. If you did, I'm sure you had a few ;). Talk about one or more and try to color in periods that you blacked out with fun elaboration.

140. Talk about your first (or most memorable) parental visit experience during college. All the awkwardness and the explanation that needs to occur can make these some of the most important events during school. Try to recall one that was a real game-changing event.

141. Going back home from the holidays is a big part of college. Friends change, you change. Talk about an experience in which this was completely evident and what this made you think about your high school friendships and the town itself.

142. Do you feel proud to be an alumni (or will you feel proud when you've graduated) of your school? Do you watch the games and donate to the funds, etc.? Why or why not do you feel this way or do these things in relation to your school?

143. Dorm room sex. Whether you walked in on it or had it in college, it was kind of weird. Write a story about it.

144. Write a story about a college kid visiting schools and stepping into his first all-you-can-eat dining hall.

Creative Writing Prompts: Prom

145. Write a story detailing your most memorable prom (Junior, Senior, College, etc.) from top to bottom. From what you and your date wore, to whom you went with and the songs you danced to.

146. What would be the perfect "last dance" song to you? Which song could you see yourself remembering for the rest of your life for "good reasons?" Talk about how your dance with the love of your life would have been with that song playing.

147. You, your date, and your friends are all drinking inside the limo that is taking you guys to prom. Here's the problem. The limo has been pulled over

and all of you have been busted! Describe your prom evening that is taking place in the police station waiting for your parents.

148. Who was your best date ever to one of these school dances? Who was your worst date? Do a sort of back and forth story between the two, comparing what one date did correctly and what the other did...less than correctly :).

149. Oh, those parental pre-prom picture sessions. Write a story (using your experiences or not) demonstrating the wackiness of a series of photographs before the prom. What do the freeze frames look like and what is happening in between them.

150. What are the wackiest prom outfits you've ever seen? Is it the pimp outfit? The duct tape dress? Go into detail and then put yourself in the shoes of the person who wore such an outfit.

151. Imagine your senior prom...as if it were in a 1980s movie! Cast some popular stereotypes (or 80s actors) for these roles and go to town. It doesn't matter if your prom actually was in the 80s or not, as these movies didn't always...match the times anyway :).

152. Write about a girl at a prom whose dress has completely fallen apart and she needs to deal with it and either salvage or flee the prom as soon as she can. This can be from experience or not :).

153. Asking someone to the dance can be the scariest part of prom. Create a story in which a boy unsuccessfully asks 4 dates to prom before find the right one.

154. The school's favorite band is playing prom! And they've...got their own way of doing things. Imagine that you are an administrator and that your job is to keep the band in line. Explain what happens over the course of the night.

155. You have been given the power to re-write your own prom experiences to be absolutely perfect. From the pre-picture section to the after-party. What is your ideal prom?

156. Unbeknownst to you, on the other side of your prom, people that you don't even know that well were having a wild and crazy night. Go through an

old yearbook and write a potential story about at least two people you don't know all that well.

Creative Writing Prompts: Divorce

157. Create a character that experienced his parents' divorce at a very young age. How has this affected his or her trust issues and how the character feels about love as he or she has grown up?

158. If you've been divorced, write a story about your experiences going through the process from the decision all the way through the first few years. If you haven't, create a story about characters that have.

159. An inevitable part of divorce is how it affects the family, both immediate and extended. Create a story based on 2 Christmas holidays, one pre-divorce and one post-divorce. Have the entire family involved in each.

160. You and your spouse are equal friends with couple that is getting a divorce. How does this change the friendship and do you side with one particularly over another?

161. You, a recent divorcee, are going on a first date with another recent divorcee. You can't help but talk about your recently ended marriages. How does this dialogue go? Is there a second date?

162. If you were to get divorced from a significant other, do you think it would be amicable or brutal? Create a story of both possibilities if you aren't sure.

163. Detail a story of a brutal legal battle between a divorcing couple over custody and child support. It's tough stuff, but there are so many pieces of literature, television, and film about it, it's worth giving a shot.

164. You feel as though you are in an amazing marriage with an amazing partner. Out of nowhere, your partner asks for a divorce. What happens next?

165. It's tough not to gossip a little. Which two celebrities do you think will get a divorce next? You can always read the latest trashy tabloid to get some ideas :).

166. If you were a child of divorce, how do you feel like you dealt with it? Did you have to go to therapy? Did it help? I'm sure that it's hard, but extreme detail can be very beneficial.

167. You are given a magical choice. You can give your ex-spouse extreme happiness and have her find the love of her life with the push of a button. The other button, leads to her wanting to get back together with you, though your marriage troubles continue. What do you pick, why and what's the fallout?

168. Not all divorces end badly as some lead to a much less contentious relationship and better partnerships for both parties involved. Write a story about a couple that actually becomes stronger friends after having a divorce.

Creative Writing Prompts: Travel

169. What is the best vacation you've ever been on? Who were you with, where did you travel to, what were some of the sights that you saw? Write down every detail and pose a hypothetical trip with the same people if you went back today.

170. What is the worst vacation you've ever been on? What fights occurred, how lost did you get, how much money did you lose, etc.? Pose a hypothetical of the trip going perfectly and see what major things would have changed.

171. What is your most memorable airport/airplane experience? Did you sit on the runway for a long time? Talk to a runway model on the plane? Have to run...way far to get to your gate on time? :) Use lots of details and try to remember all of the emotions that you had at the time.

172. Talk about a time in which you had to show someone foreign to your neighborhood, town, country, planet around the area. Do you feel as though you were a good tour guide? What did this person (or alien) think after your demonstration?

173. Create a story in which you are in a foreign country in which you don't speak the language...and you've lost all of your belongings (cash included). How do you deal with this situation?

174. Why is travel so stressful? What would you have to do to take all of the stress out of traveling for yourself? A closer airport? Calmer family members? Your own jet? Talk about it as if it was happening and detail your first stress-free traveling experience.

175. Did you ever have a foreign love experience? If not, make one up and talk about how you met, how your love progressed, and what it was like leaving him or her (if you ever did leave!).

176. Have you ever traveled back to the "mother country" to discover your family's roots? If not, make up a story in which you did and see how much you can find out about your ancestry. Did you learn anything about yourself and the kind of person you are on this trip?

177. Talk about a road trip that you've had. Who was there, where were you going, and what seedy rest stops did you go to along the way? If you haven't been on such a trip, create the ideal trip for yourself by getting your best friends together and going to your favorite drivable location (that is at least 100 miles away).

178. You are in the airport and you are about to travel home for the holidays. Except one problem: you're snowed in! Talk about your night (or nights) at the airport and if you meet any strange and interesting people.

179. You have been granted the ability to fly! I mean, like Superman! Where do you travel with this newfound ability now that you don't need to save up frequent flyer miles?

180. You have put together your dream travelling team of living and deceased people. Who are they and where do you go?

Creative Writing Prompts: Regrets

181. Talk about the biggest regret you've had in your entire life. What led up to this occurring and what was the aftermath? What have you learned from this situation and how have you applied it to what you do now?

182. Do a character study on a person who uses his regrets to guide most of the decisions he makes in his life. What would happen to this person if he was able to move on free of these past transgressions?

183. What is one way that you have dealt with the regrets in your life? Do you just let them go easily or does it take a lot of talking and time? Have you needed to get professional help? Discuss the entire process for working regret out of your system.

184. What would you do if you could reverse one major regret from your past? How do you think your life would change if this was erased and how would it affect you as a person? Was it really all that much of an impact?

185. Go back in your mind to a conversation that you wish had not gotten so emotional and change it into a logical discussion on your part. Word for word, alter what was said and turn it into an empathic and emotional discourse. How does it change and what is the end result?

186. You have been given one last day with the "one that got away." What do you do with this time, what do you say, and what do you do? You only have this one last chance, so make it count.

187. Imagine that you have had a negative conversation with a person who passed away before you were able to make up. Write about the situation and your attempts to communicate with this person beyond the grave.

188. Write down a plan for your future financial situations based on the poor decisions that you have made in the past. Instead of regretting these past problems, try to look at them as opportunities to move forward with this new knowledge.

189. Craft a story about a kid who made a mistake in elementary school that cost him his popularity through middle and high school. Then give him an opportunity to go back and change that mistake. He can then choose between these two paths for the rest of his life. What path does he choose and why?

190. Have you ever caused extreme harm to someone without knowing it and then found out years later about what was said or done? If so, write about that experience, if not, create a story in which someone from your past comes up to confront you about said past issue.

191. Create a giant chart of all the major regrets of your life and write a story in which you rectify all of these wrongs. It's sort of like the show "My Name is Earl." Go into detail and try to fix everything from childhood through adulthood.

192. Talk about something that you used to regret but that upon thinking about it you have actually learned a great lesson.

Creative Writing Prompts: Memory

193. What is your earliest childhood memory? What do you think was going on around your memory that you don't quite remember? Would you have changed this memory if you could?

194. You have suddenly been given enhanced brain power and you can remember everything that's ever happened to you nearly at the same time. What do you remember that causes you to change how you behave currently? What are some lessons you learned that you promptly forgot?

195. You and a significant other are recounting the story of how you met to a couple of friends. How do your stories differ and explain why you think that is.

196. If you could change one memory for the better, what would it be and why? Go into extreme detail including the context and subtext of everything going on during this unfortunate memory.

197. Trace the origins of one of your habits. For example: Why do you kiss your hand and touch the roof of your car every time you go through a yellow light? Did you have a friend who started doing that and you followed her lead? Figure out when you started doing something that you now do all the time.

198. You have just gotten in a car accident and have complete and total amnesia. How do you cope with this and how do the people around you attempt to jog your memory back to working condition?

199. You have to deal with a parent who is suffering through Alzheimer's disease. What do you do to preserve the ailing memory of your mom or dad and how do you deal with the emotions that you're experiencing?

200. If you could forget one memory that haunts you, what would it be and why? Go into extreme detail including the context and subtext of everything going on during this memory. How would life change once you've forgotten it?

201. Create a story of how you enhanced your brain power over 100% using nutritional supplements, exercises, and a whole lot of hard work. Perhaps creating this story actually will improve your brain!

202. Remember back to an extremely happy time in your life. Write down as many details as you can remember about the time, including what you were wearing, how the room was decorated, what it smelled like, etc.

203. If you could switch brains with any one person who would it be? Keep in mind (ha!) that you may lose your memories and they would be replaced by this person's.

204. You run into a friend who was involved in one of your most vivid memories. You bring up the story and your friend remembers it completely differently. Chat about your stories until you determine the real events that occurred.

Creative Writing Prompts: Time

205. You have been given a time machine and can travel to any point in the history of the Earth. Where will you travel and why? What is your first week like in this new time period?

206. Theories of time and space go (as far as my understanding at least :)) that if you travel at the speed of light, you will not age while the rest of the world goes on at normal time. Imagine that you have gone on a journey and come back to Earth to find that ten years have passed. All of your friends, family, and favorite restaurants have aged ten years. How does this change the way you live your life?

207. If you could fast forward ahead or rewind backwards to any point in your life, what would it be and why? Be very detailed about how you deal with this second chance or sneak peak.

208. What would you do if you had control over space and time (like Hiro Nakamura in the television show "Heroes")? Would you use it to help people or just to get everything that you want? Talk about your first full day with this power and how it changes things.

209. Spend a week making a list of how much time you spend on given activities. Using this, create a story of you crafting your ideal week in which you spend every waking moment doing something productive or exciting. You can skip work, try something new, and spend time with the ones you love. Just be very specific. Then think to yourself, "Is there any way I can actually do this in my real life?"

210. Create a story with a character that is obsessed with time. His house is full of clocks and his arms are covered in watches. Describe his daily routines to make sure that he is hyper aware of every second that passes.

211. As of the writing of this prompt, daylight savings is on its way (Fall back!). What is the best way for you to possibly spend one extra hour in your week? Craft a tale in which you (or a character) use that hour to the best of your ability.

212. They say timing is everything. How would your life change if you had perfect timing? You'd always say and do things at exactly the perfect time without fail. How will things improve for you? Be specific.

213. You have been given an unlimited grant by a fancy millionaire to do what it is you do best for 40 hours a week. What do you do with this newfound freedom? How does it change your life?

214. The world begins to move for you in slow-motion. You have the ability to notice things right as they are happening (catching objects that are falling, moving out of the way of danger, etc). How does this change things for you? Where did this ability come from? Craft an origin story and a day in the life.

215. You have been granted a new position as a sort of Time FBI agent (similarly to many movies). You have to chase villains who are trying to mess with the natural timeline for financial and social gain. Talk about at least one of your missions (if not many of them).

216. If time is money, what do you deserve to be paid per hour and why?

Creative Writing Prompts: History

217. Imagine that you are the right hand man of Alexander the Great as he makes his conquest through the world. What do you guys talk about late at night when everybody has gone to sleep?

218. Suppose for a second that reincarnation exists and write a history of all the past lives you have lived and how they currently affect you.

219. Put yourself in the place of one of the greatly oppressed people of all history. You are on the cusp of an uprising and you must sacrifice everything for the cause. What do you do to make the world a better place for your people?

220. Re-write a boring event from history (like the signing of some random law) and turn it into a wild event with magic, intrigue and mystery.

221. Pretend that you are a sadistic history teacher who decides to make up the history of an imaginary nation for his children and test them on it. What is the nation and what is their history?

222. What is the period of history that you identify with the most? The flappers of the American 1920's? The royal family during the War of the Roses? Choose one and write a day in the life for yourself during that time.

223. You have stumbled upon a history book from an alien realm with thousands of years of history behind them. How does their history compare with ours?

224. You and a friend are having a conversation when he brings up an event he believes really happened in history. Funny thing is… the event was completely made up in a movie! Detail the conversation of you trying to convince him the error of his ways.

225. What do you think a history book 200 years from now will say about the current generation and its innovations?

226. How do you want to be remembered in history? What would they say about you in a history textbook and what chapter would it be in?

227. Imagine that you were present for several great moments of history. For example: the discovery of fire, the creation of the polio cure and the destruction of the Berlin Wall. How did those events go down? Try writing

these scenes in several different styles: comedic, tragic, farcical or however you decide.

228. Who is the strangest historical figure you can think of? Write a day in his life.

Creative Writing Prompts: Archaeology

229. You are a half action hero, half archaeologist like Indiana Jones. What quests do you take on and what kind of ancient civilizations do you attempt to unearth secrets from?

230. What do you feel is the most interesting and varied ancient culture? Which one would you choose if you could only study one people and one language? Now imagine a day in the life of a normal person in this culture far in the past. What would be the typical daily activities for this person?

231. You are in class with one of the most important scholars of archaeology in the whole world. Lucky you! What do you believe this person would tell you about archaeology and why it is such an integral study for you to understand the world?

232. What part of ancient cultures do you find the most interesting? The literature? The music? What do you feel it is you can understand from these civilizations by getting a feel for this part of the culture?

233. Craft a story about a team of archaeologists making a great discovery at a dig site. Not only is it an important discovery but it becomes a majorly big deal throughout the world and tells us something integral about our current way of life. What is it and what is it like touring the discovery all over the planet.

234. You are an archaeologist at a dig site and you find what must be the ancient version of you in an old uncovered house. All the things of this person's life seem to overlap with your own. You enjoy parallel leisure activities, have the same ways of going about problems, and the same goals. What can you learn from yourself by learning from this person?

235. One thousand years in the future your house has been excavated by archeologists. What do they find out about your life and how do they interpret you in comparison to the rest of humanity that was living during your era?

236. Look around you wherever you are. Plot back over the course of thousands of years, listing what you believe was in your current location every hundred years or so. Create a series of stories based on the people who lived there during those previous generations.

237. Talk about some things that you've learned about ancient cultures from trips to other countries (or other parts of your country). Turn these pieces of knowledge into a Dan Brown-esque adventure story where people must discover clues throughout history to solve a major world crisis.

238. In your basement you have discovered an ancient scroll that pretty much reveals the meaning of life. Who created this scroll and how did they come up with such an answer? What do you do with the scroll thereafter?

239. You have become the leader of the ancient civilization of your choice. Which civilization do you choose and what do you do during your reign that will stand the test of time?

240. Describe a day in the life of an ancient human.

4 LIFE

Creative Writing Prompts: Work

241. In a magical turn of events, you have become the boss of your office. Your former boss now has the position you had and you get to control both the direction of the company and how you treat your employees. How do you change the faults of the previous boss and do you let power change you at all? Be honest!

242. It's the office Christmas party and you have had one too many. What do you do with your lack of inhibitions and with all your co-workers as an arm's length?

243. Time for some inter-office gossip...about you! Write a conversation of three people at work talking about you behind your back. Feel free to make the rumors progressively more ridiculous as you go on.

244. What is your dream job? Talk about how to get it and what you do when you have it. Go into enough detail and maybe it will come true :).

245. Who is your work crush? You know what I'm talking about. The most-attractive person there who you lavish most of your attention on. Talk about this person and what makes him or her so compelling. Feel free to add a love story to the end of it.

246. You have been laid off. What do you do to make ends meet and is there any way you can use this event to get into a better situation than you originally were?

247. You become involved in a conspiracy to rip-off your company! How did you get into this situation and are you going to follow through with it? Does your conspiracy end up getting away with it?

248. You have been given a huge raise. I'm talking about double the money you are making right now. What do you do with your new found cash flow?

249. Detail a night of you out with your work friends (if you don't have any, just your co-workers). The night is long and full of alcohol and may involve the spilling of many secrets. What do you learn? What do you tell?

250. You give the best presentation of your life about the thing you care about the most in this world. Write down the presentation as if you were actually going to present it.

251. The fairy godmother of the working world has come knocking on your door, ready to grant you three wishes that can only take place in your present job and during the hours of 9 to 5. What do you wish for and how does it turn out?

252. Author Robert G. Allen talked about creating multiple streams of income. What would your extra sources of income you had unlimited time and resources to create them?

Creative Writing Prompts: Home

253. What does the concept of home mean to you? Would you call just one place or multiple places home at this time? Describe how you came to this feeling about your "home."

254. What are the things you always look forward to when you're home? Are there certain places you like to eat at? Certain people that you like to see? What activities do you do? Be very specific.

255. Would you still consider the place you grew up as being home? If so, talk about all the things that still make it a place to come back to. If not, determine the events that led up to it losing its status.

256. Write a story in which you are unemployed and you lose your physical home. Where do you go and what do you do? Is there any place in the world that you still refer to as "home?" How do you keep yourself from feeling lost and despaired?

257. Imagine that you are a child of divorce that must go between two parents' houses due to joint custody. Which house do you consider to be home and why? Talk about a situation in which you tell both of your parents this and how they react.

258. Do you look forward to coming "home" for the holidays? What kind of preparations does your family make in order to make you feel more at home? Is there a place that you would rather be to enjoy yourself more during this typically family-filled time of the year?

259. If you could choose any place to be your home; to be a place that you felt comfortable in and could enjoy most of your days where would it be? Feel free to choose anywhere in the world, even if it's somewhere you haven't been.

260. Do you have a restaurant, bar, or other hangout that you feel is your home away from home? It's the kind of place where everybody knows your name, like the show "Cheers." The kind of place where they'd ask about you if you didn't show up for a couple of days. Talk about how this became such a location for you.

261. Do you have a group of friends that you always hang out with when you're home? Do you ever find yourself slipping back into old habits and mannerisms when this occurs? Compare a hangout from a long time ago with these home friends with what a hangout would consist of right now.

262. Talk about accomplishing something that you always wanted to do in and around your home. Is it asking out that old high school crush, going to that one tourist place you never got around to, supporting that one local cause? Imagine achieving this task with flying colors and how it makes you feel.

263. Have you ever seen that Twilight Zone episode where the little boy gets magical powers that allow him to hear everybody's thoughts and change people into toys if he doesn't like where their thoughts are going? You have been given such powers in and around your home. Do you use them for evil or good? How does it all go down?

264. It's been ten years since you've been home and you show up at your parents' doorstep. What happens next?

Creative Writing Prompts: Success

265. What is your number one goal in life? If you do not yet have one, no time like now to choose it :). How do you plan on reaching this goal? What would happen if you achieved it? What would be the next step?

266. Talk about a time in which you felt really accomplished. This could be any number of things. Go into extreme detail, especially about your emotions surrounding the event. How did other people feel about your achievement?

267. Have you ever felt jealous from someone else's success? Who was this person and why did it affect you so much? Would you change your reaction to this situation if you could?

268. Who is the most successful person you know? What can you learn from this person that is applicable to your own life? Write about a meeting with this big achiever in which you learn all of his or her secrets.

269. If you could have a meeting with any success guru (a la Tony Robbins or Rhonda Byrne) who would it be and why? What would you talk to them about and how could you learn more about your life through them?

270. Talk about a time in your life where you felt like a failure. What did you learn from this experience that may have helped you to become a stronger person?

271. Write a story about a person rising through the ranks of your field (it could be writing, advertising, anything really). Detail his or her rise from the bottom of a field to the top of it. Are there any steps this fictional person took that you could take yourself?

272. What is the definition of success to you? Is it the absence of failure? Keep in mind that failure allows you to learn things, so if "the absence of failure" is your definition, try to revise it to be more positive and achievable. Write a few different definitions before you settle on one that's right for you. Then apply it to your life and talk about ways in which this definition could help.

273. Talk about the ways in which you are a success and the ways in which you are not. Go into extreme detail with every part of your life. How could you become more successful in some of the areas that are lacking?

274. Do your parents view you as a success? If they weren't around or passed away prematurely, do you think they'd be happy with your success wherever they may be? Talk about that and discuss if it matters or not.

275. You have encountered a Success Genie who will grant you three wishes to make your life more successful. He won't give you ten billion dollars or suddenly make you look super attractive, but he will add to the success of your life. What will your three wishes be and talk about your encounter with the genie as a whole.

276. If you had a choice between the success and happiness of your partner or the success and happiness of yourself, which would you choose? Describe a day in the life after your choice has occurred.

Creative Writing Prompts: Love

277. Start a story or script by repeating the name of the love of your life twice before anything else.

278. You wake up suddenly to find the "one that got away" sleeping quietly beside you. First thoughts that come to your mind.

279. You walk into your apartment or house to find your greatest love and your best friend are undressing each other on the kitchen floor. How do you react?

280. Re-enact your first date with the love of your life.

281. You have just recognized the girl or guy in the elevator with you. She/he is the person you loved from afar in high school but never asked out. The elevator stops between floors. You two are alone and stuck for at least an hour. What do you do?

282. The person who completely broke your heart is meeting you for coffee in an hour. Describe the next three hours.

283. Your most awkward, embarrassing school dance. Go! :)

284. Your best first kiss, the lead up, and the aftermath.

285. You and your secret crush debate the topic, "better to have loved and lose then to have never loved at all."

286. Losing your virginity, the lead up, and the aftermath.

287. Use the words of a song that make you think of the one who got away as a frame for a story that shows you going through a box of old things.

288. You sit down for lunch with the Devil. Yes, the Devil! He gives you a choice: to spend the rest of your life with the man or woman who got away but you lose your soul, or you keep your soul but you will never have another chance with that person. Weigh both options in your head, decide, deal with your choice.

289. Your best friend within your sexual preference has just declared his or her long-standing feelings for you. Describe the conversation that follows.

290. After casual sex with your office or classroom crush, your crush says the words, "I love you." What happens then?

291. You are waiting for the love of your life to walk down the aisle. Your love's mother comes in with a note. He or she has gotten cold feet. Describe dealing with the two families afterwards and the resulting emotions.

292. Describe a trip outside of your home country that you took with a romantic partner.

293. Describe a memorable drug or alcohol experience that you had with a romantic partner.

294. Imagine that the person who broke your heart the most came crawling back. How would you react?

295. The most passionate intimate or sexual experience of your life! Have fun with this one.

296. The first time you told a non-family member that wonderful and scary phrase, "I love you." The lead up and the aftermath.

Creative Writing Prompts: Death

297. You have just walked up to the open casket of your favorite grandparent. How does it make you feel?

298. Your best friend has just been in a horrible accident and is on life support, possibly for the rest of his or her life. Your friend has appointed you to be the person who pulls the plug for his or her Do Not Resuscitate order. Describe your feelings.

299. Your grandmother just passed away and she personally left you $100,000. Do you do something in her memory or spend it on yourself? Start the story from the reading of the will.

300. While waiting for a train, a large man in a hooded sweatshirt asks you for change. You give him a dollar and you walk to the far side of the platform. He follows and then pulls a gun on you. Start from there.

301. Your partner has died in a sudden accident and you have to deliver the main eulogy. Detail your process of creating this eulogy while grieving.

302. You are watching your own viewing from the back of the room. Who eulogizes you and what do they say? (Thanks to Stephen Covey for the inspiration for this!)

303. Your favorite pet is ailing incredibly. The vet says that he could survive up to one more year but in increasingly worse pain. He suggests putting the pet down. Describe what you do.

304. The plane you are flying in begins to lose cabin pressure rapidly. You are told to prepare for emergency landing procedure. What do you do?

305. You have been diagnosed with terminal cancer. Describe your first week after finding this out.

306. Your friend or spouse is in the third trimester of pregnancy. Due to complications, she must choose between the baby and herself. She is leaning towards choosing the baby. How do you advise her?

307. You see a little boy wander into the middle of a busy intersection. What do you do?

308. Your father has told you that he is in incredible pain and that he wants you to help him kill himself. What do you say or do?

309. You see a homeless man lying by the side of a building. You are not sure if he is dead or sleeping. Go from there.

310. You are the witness of a group beating that is in progress. What do you see? What do you do?

311. You wake up to find yourself bleeding profusely and you aren't sure from where. You will definitely need medical attention. Describe your next few hours.

312. You are in an extremely heated argument with your partner. He or she goes tumbling down the stairs. Your partner is not moving or responding. Describe the next few hours.

313. You have just been informed that the discomfort you felt earlier in the day was a mild heart attack. What will you do to change your lifestyle?

314. Your father has just passed away. Describe dealing with your mother.

315. Your elderly grandmother has been trying to complete an extensive family scrapbook for years, but she has become too frail. You decide to help her out. Describe the process of creating this work with your grandmother.

316. You are on your deathbed, surrounded by your loved ones. They are attentively waiting what may be your final words. Describe the scene, what you say, and the last precious moments of life.

Creative Writing Prompts: Family

317. Recall and write a detailed account of your most embarrassing moment with your mother, step-mother, or other mother like figure.

318. Describe the time around the moment you realized that your mother and father were in fact not perfect or normal.

319. Write a story of your older brother or sister beating you up or you beating up a younger brother or sister. If it never happened, make it up.

320. Describe this event: finding out the true nature of Santa Claus or the Easter Bunny and your first confrontation with your parents afterward.

321. In a detailed manner, write about the day of and the day after your little brother or sister was born.

322. You just realized (at whatever age this happened) that your parents do indeed have sex. Write about how you found out, your reaction, and the ensuing time you speak with your parents.

323. Evaluate your place with your entire family. The starving artist? The slacker? The underachieving genius? Label your role and start labeling the other members of your family as well. Explain the labels.

324. Describe your most memorable family holiday/vacation.

325. Describe the first time you introduced a boyfriend or girlfriend to your immediate family.

326. Describe the first time you introduced a boyfriend or girlfriend to your extended family.

327. Use research or imagination to write a day in the life story of your mother, father or siblings when they were your current age.

328. In a "Freaky Friday"-esque situation, you have switched bodies with your mother or father. Describe your next 24 hours.

329. Write a story of one of your ancestors in connection to a famous event in history.

330. Think back to an event with your family from your childhood. Write a scene between you and a parent or sibling and try to piece together the whole event.

331. Either remember back to or imagine if your parents were to tell you that they were getting a divorce, describe your next 24 hours.

332. How did your sibling's reputation affect how teachers treated you in school (or vice versa)? Describe specific situations.

333. You have to spend a week with one cousin, who do you choose and why? Describe the week.

334. You have to spend a week with one grandparent or one pairing of grandparents. Who do you choose and why? Describe the week.

335. Describe your family's greatest catastrophe to date.

336. Imagine or describe your own wedding and the involvement of your family in the planning and execution.

Creative Writing Prompts: Friendship

337. Your best friend in the world calls you and tells you a secret that changes your friendship forever. Describe the conversation and the aftermath.

338. Detail the scene of the first time you told your friends you had a crush on somebody. Did they react negatively or poorly? Did their reaction affect how you handled yourself around this person?

339. The friend you are most disappointed that you had a falling out with knocks on your door. He or she comes in and you two sit down and talk about the old times and the new times. Write the conversation.

340. A woman or man you have been dating for the past few months says that she or he does not want to ever hang out with your friends ever again. How do you handle the situation?

341. The craziest experience you've ever shared with your friends. Go!

342. Look back in your life for a time when you had a bad breakup and you went to your friends for help. What happened?

343. You are asked to testify against a good friend of yours in a court case. Your friend is being tried for murder. You know full well that he committed it. What do you do?

344. What was it like the first time you introduced one of your high school friends to your college friends and versa?

345. Remember a time where two of your friends began to date. If this didn't happen, make up a story in which it did. How does it play out?

346. Your first major fight with a friend. The lead-up and the aftermath.

347. Your last major fight with your best friend. The lead-up and the aftermath.

348. Your friend is dating a horrible, horrible person. How do you deal with it? If this situation has happened in your life, feel free to draw from that.

349. You are lab partners with your friend in a science class. She is doing absolutely no work and she's bringing your grade down. How do you approach her about it?

350. During a drunken party, you and a friend made-out, fooled around or had sexual intercourse. Describe the encounter and the following day. Once again, if this has actually happened, use it.

351. A friend has borrowed a large sum of money from you and has yet to repay it. How do you approach the situation?

352. You come over to the house of some friends and realize you have walked straight into an intervention! What is the intervention about and how would you honestly react? Don't make this your ideal nice person reaction, be truthful.

353. A body has been found and the dental records show it is your best friend. The parents have asked you to go and identify the body. Describe the experience.

354. Look in your life for a time that you and a good friend were roommates. How did this situation turn out? Beginning, middle and end.

355. Your best friend calls you while crying up a storm. How do you comfort your friend and what is it probably about?

356. Describe meeting your best friend in the world.

Creative Writing Prompts: Pregnancy

357. Imagine that you have become pregnant accidentally. What are the thoughts that run through your head and what decisions do you make about your life from there on out? What do the people in your life say to you as advice?

358. Write about walking around during the 8th and 9th month of pregnancy while carrying around this extremely heavy baby in your womb. Talk about it during your first pregnancy, making it the first experience with this for you. How do you feel and what activities are you extremely restricted from.

359. What is your experience with the mood shifts of pregnancy? Were you able to keep them under control or did you sometimes have burst of emotions that affected the people around you? How did you and those people cope with said emotions?

360. Discuss the experience of having life inside of you. How does it make you feel and is there any other experience that you can compare it to? Be very detailed.

361. You are going into labor! Describe the whirlwind of rushing to the hospital (or rushing to your birthing site) and giving birth. Did you choose to take drugs or not? Did you need to get a C-section or not? Talk about everything.

362. Did people treat you differently in a good way or a bad way when they found that you were pregnant? Did you find that you were able to relate more to some and less to others? How did work, home, and public times in your life change?

363. How do you feel that you were similar and different to when your mother was pregnant with you? How does she discuss it and what do you think that you could do differently to make it a better experience for you?

364. Talk about the people that have helped you during your pregnancy. Whether they are friends, family, or significant others, write about the ways in which they were indispensable during your 9 months of pregnancy.

365. Imagine that you are a little boy or girl and you have just found out that your mother is pregnant again. How does this affect you? Play this against a story in which you find out about the pregnancy of yourself or a significant other. How are they different and how are they similar?

366. Go into detail about all the preparations for a baby. Picking out the furniture, getting clothing, coming up with names, etc. Have fun with this, especially if you've never been pregnant before or if you're an old pro.

367. You have a choice of giving birth to a clone of any famous person living or dead and bringing them up through their youth. Who do you choose and how do things change with the knowledge of the great potential this baby has?

368. Imagine that you have accidentally become pregnant. How would it change your current lifestyle and what would you do as a result?

Creative Writing Prompts: Babies

369. Imagine that you are to start your life over from the age of an infant. How would you change things as you grow up?

370. Write a story from the perspective of a baby as he is being born.

371. Write a story from the perspective of a third-party watching a baby's birth.

372. There are many different theories about how a baby should be raised. How do you feel that a baby should be brought up so as to be both safe and prepared for the world at large?

373. Talk about the first time you ever held a baby. What did it feel like and what were the circumstances that led up to it?

374. Talk about what it means or what it will mean to be a father or a mother for the first time.

375. If you had first-hand knowledge that giving up your career and tending to a baby would cause a great improvement in your baby's life, would you do it and why?

376. Tell a story about your baby's first trip to the doctor's office either from your perspective or from the perspective of the baby.

377. One of the greatest fears a soon-to-be parent has is that his child will have a mental or physical disability. Do you believe that the field of genetics should attempt to cure such problems with test-tube babies and genetic manipulation? Why or why not?

378. Your baby has learned to crawl and has caused a ton of havoc in just a few short hours. Describe the scene and go into extreme detail about the mess your baby has caused.

379. Create a conversation between a bunch of infants at a playgroup meeting.

380. Do you feel as though you are (or will be) similar to your child as your parents were toward you when you were a baby? Were they the model parents and were you the model baby?

Creative Writing Prompts: Prosperity

381. Imagine that you have a $100 bill in your wallet. You go to the grocery store and after making purchases you spend exactly $100. When you look back in your wallet you see that there is another $100. You spend it again. It comes back! Detail your first week with this ever-replenishing $100 bill (Thanks to the Hicks' and Steve Pavlina for this idea).

382. You have just won a great sum of money from the lottery to be divvied out in $1000 increments each week for the rest of your life. What will you do

with this newly added income? Describe your first year with this exciting addition to your life.

383. After a freak accident (resembling a comic book origin story) you gain the ability to receive everything that you think about. How do you use this newfound power to increase your money, your possessions, and your charity?

384. Your hard work on a screenplay has paid off! Not have you sold your first one for $500,000, but a powerful Hollywood executive has asked you to complete a 5 picture deal, making double that amount on each progressive script. Talk about the changes in your life that have occurred from this new offer. How does this change your family, friends, and living arrangements?

385. A wealthy relative has passed away, leaving you her entire estate. She asks that you use this money to secure your future and to improve the conditions of the community she grew up in. Talk about the step by step plan you create and how people around you react to your decisions.

386. A few strokes of luck have propelled you through the social ranks. You now call several big celebrities your friends and they have given you enough opportunities to make almost ten times the money you make now. How do you balance this new social lifestyle with your work and home life?

387. You have $100,000 to give to whatever charities you want. Pick, choose, and visit each of these charities directly, getting a chance to see exactly where your money has gone.

388. It suddenly comes to you, the idea that will make you financially stable and secure for the rest of your life. The only problem? You have to majorly renovate your life to be more productive and efficient. What will you do? Can you successfully avoid Buffy the Vampire Slayer reruns to get your idea in place effectively?

389. Your significant other becomes a millionaire and starts buying stuff for you all the time. How does that make you feel? Can you use your lessons to become wealthy yourself?

390. The greatest financial minds of all time have taken you into a big conference room. You have the opportunity to ask them as many questions as you want; to learn their secrets. What do you ask them and who tells you what?

391. You are somehow transported back into the 1940s with a million dollars in your bank account. That practically makes you a billionaire compared to the 2000s. What will you do with your time now that you can pretty much buy anything you want (that has been created by the 1940s :)) ?

392. What makes a person deserve prosperity? Do you feel as though you've earned that right?

Creative Writing Prompts: Manhood

393. You're going to poker night! Whether you want to or not. You're going to be hanging out with some real "guys' guys" for the next 5 hours with lots of beer, smoking, and dirty language. How'd you get roped into this and how does the experience sit with you?

394. You are sitting down on a bench at the mall while your significant other goes off to his/her 4th shop of the day. You are trying to organize the several bags he/she's left you with when an older man sits down next to you with bags of his own. You strike up a conversation and talk about what it's like being a married man. Write the entire conversation here.

395. Your first sexual experience. Be honest! If you haven't had one, make it up or create what your ideal first sexual encounter would be like.

396. You are in the midst of hell week at a fraternity. You have just been blindfolded and thrown into a van with several other pledges. What do you guys talk about during the ride to this unknown location? Feel free to continue the story throughout the night that follows.

397. You are very intoxicated at a bar and you completely black out. You wake up the next day with an unknown partner in your bed. How do you deal with the situation and what do you tell your friends who were at the bar with you?

398. Explain what exercise and physical fitness means to you as a man. Are you the type to build up your muscles with protein powder with creatine? The kind who runs 50 miles a week? The kind who doesn't do anything? Why? And what is your ideal physical condition?

399. It happens to everybody, or so they say. You have begun to have trouble getting an erection. How do you cope with this? How does this affect your life and your opinion of yourself?

400. Bonding time with Dad! You and your father go out fishing, camping, or something else outdoorsy and he gives you some fatherly advice about life. What do you talk about and has this wisdom affected you? Could be a true story or completely made up.

401. You have just had your first child! How does this change your normal life and how do you and your significant other split the time taking care of him?

402. You have just walked into the pornography section of your local video store. While trying to keep a low profile, you walk right into your boss! Describe the hilariously awkward conversation that ensues.

403. You are playing your favorite video game with your three best friends. One of them says, "I love you guys." How do you react? Describe the conversation that follows.

404. What makes you a man? What are some properties you would use to describe someone who is manly?

5 HEALTH

Creative Writing Prompts: Health

405. Write a story about a time that you were injured, whether it was a small injury or a more serious one. How did you deal with the problem and what kind of medical attention did you receive? If it was a long time ago and you don't quite remember, fill in some made-up details.

406. What is the most sick you have ever been? What caused it and what did you have to do to recover? Go into the deep and gross detail, as you may get some effective new ways to describe things from such an exercise.

407. Talk about a time in which you avoided Western medicine and found a cure with alternative methods. Some of these methods might include herbal remedies, acupuncture, Qi Gong, etc. If you have never done anything like that, do a bit of research and craft a story involving such practices.

408. Write about your favorite and least favorite doctors throughout your lifetime. What made them memorable as the best and the worst that you have had treat you. Create a conversation between the three of you all at the same time, where you try to get the bad doctors to understand a better way of doing things.

409. Detail a story that draws from an experience in which you had to care for someone who was ill or injured. How did you help him or her to feel better and what did you learn in the process?

410. Have you ever feared for your life during an injury or illness? Talk about those feelings and if you haven't, create a story in which you felt close to death. What happened and how did you make a complete recovery?

411. There are so many reports of deaths, injuries, and illnesses on the news; it sometimes feels like we're desensitized to everything. What was one news story that truly affected you and made you think differently about your own life? If none has, pick a headline and run with it.

412. Put yourself as a character into any television, movie, or book medical drama. What do you add to the hospital or private practice and what kind of medical knowledge have you instilled your character with? Have fun with this one.

413. Create a character (or draw from your own experiences) with a chronic pain or illness that requires daily maintenance. How does it change his life and how does he keep a positive attitude throughout it all? Is a cure possible?

414. Talk about a time in which Cancer affected your life or the lives of those around you. How would you deal with it if you were diagnosed yourself? I know this is a heavy one, but you can really get some good emotional material from such a prompt.

415. You have been given a magical healing ability to heal various wounds and illnesses. How do you go about implementing your power throughout your family and community?

416. Many people worry about what their health will be like in their old age. Describe an ideal day in the life for yourself when you are 80. Then describe one for 100 and 120 as well.

Creative Writing Prompts: Food

417. Describe the most memorable meal you've ever had in your whole life (good or bad). Go into detail of the people who were there with you (if any), the courses that were served, the location of the meal, and how you felt before and after.

418. Depending on what type of meal (good or bad) you chose in prompt #1, go the opposite direction, and describe a meal that had the opposite effect on

you. Go into the same detail of the people, courses, location, and feelings that you had.

419. Detail a fantastical evening in which you create the perfect meal, the perfect ambiance, and invite the perfect people. Elaborate greatly on the preparation and the reactions of your esteemed guests.

420. Write about eating an entire bowl of fruit. Feel free to make the fruits as exotic and interesting as possible. Really play on the use of all five senses with this exercise.

421. Your significant other (or a good friend) has invited you over for...pretty much the worst smelling and tasting meal you've ever experienced. Describe the entire encounter including every stomach churning bite.

422. This is a fun one: go into extreme (sexy) detail about a sexual encounter you've had that involved food. If you do not have such experience to draw from, make it up. If you are still stuck, watch that scene from Top Gun and you'll know what I'm talking about :).

423. You have been roped into cooking for 100 people! Describe your day from the trip to the supermarket all the way through to the interminable clean up.

424. Though the book "Cloudy with a Chance of Meatballs" is fiction...giant portions of food begin raining down from the sky! How do you spend your first week in this new world where hunger is a memory and umbrellas are a necessity?

425. There's always that dish that "momma" made better than anybody else. It's something that you can't help but associate with home. Talk about the meal (or meals) that she created and what the memory of those meals means to you.

426. If you have ever been on a diet, write about your experiences with it. If not, make up a story in which you had to go on a diet for medical reasons. What would you have to cut out and how would you cope with these changes?

427. Create a science fiction or fantasy story using the scary sounding ingredients from a package of candy or ice cream!

428. Describe you and your friends/family as foods. Go into at least five different people and describe what kinds of food they represent and why.

Creative Writing Prompts: Diet

429. You have been dieting for two weeks and you are about to step on the scale for the first time since you decided to go on this crazy thing. Write a story in which there are several alternate realities. One for losing one pound, one for losing five pounds, and one for gaining nine pounds.

430. Talk about your most memorable dieting experience? Was it a trendy thing like Atkins or South Beach or did you try to do something on your own? If you've never dieted, ask a few friends and you're bound to find somebody who has experienced a memorable diet.

431. You are on a diet and all food begins to talk to you. Of course, all the bad for you food sounds really charismatic while the diet food sounds like that date you want to leave at the restaurant. How do you deal with this awesome sounding but awful for you food?

432. You have lost the weight you've always dreamed of! Now what? Talk about how you're going to keep it off and live the life you want to live.

433. Detail using much description the eating of a plate of vegetables and brown rice versus your favorite meal ever.

434. Talk about your experiences with a weight-loss group like Weight Watchers or Jenny Craig. If you have never met with one of these groups, just make it up and see what happens. Talk about the first meeting, and the progression of good or bad advice that's given out.

435. Imagine that you have somehow gained superstardom and financial freedom. You hire a nutritionist, a trainer, and an herbalist to get you in super great shape. How does the first month of this new guided diet and exercise plan go?

436. You know that point in a diet where pretty much all food other than what you're eating looks fantastic? Detail a day in the life of a person who is going through that point.

437. You and your friends are holding an intervention for a chronic over-dieter. How does it go and what do you guys tell the person about his or her habits?

438. If you are thinking of starting a diet, write down here a plan and a story of how your first week would go. Try to make it a comedy instead of a tragedy if you actually want to follow the diet :).

439. You have been given the ability to instill extreme nutritional value into any food you wish. Which foods do you alter and what are their new properties after you change them?

440. Write a dieting horror story. It can be serious, satirical or just plain silly.

Creative Writing Prompts: Exercise

441. What is the most exercise you've ever done in one sitting? Talk about the situation that led up to this much exercise (whether intentional or unplanned). How did you feel afterward?

442. What role does exercise play in your life? Do you use it to feel better about yourself or look better? Do you avoid it at every cost? Write about a day in which you have to drastically change your amount of exercise and how it affects you.

443. Write a story about your experiences in high school gym class. Try to write from as many different points of view as possible. The overweight kid, the hotter than thou cheerleader, the perfect athlete and nice guy, the pothead, etc. Have fun with this one and all the archetypes you can pull from.

444. Craft a tale about your experiences in a gym that you felt completely out of place in. What kind of people did you see working out in there? What kind of vibe did you get from it? Detail working out there for a week and your experiences there.

445. Imagine that you have been somehow transported into the body of an extremely muscular body builder. How do people look at you as you go walking down the street? How do people look at you and interact with you when you exercise at the gym or out running? How is this different from your current life?

446. Imagine that you have been somehow transported into the body of an extremely out of shape person. How do people look at you as you go walking down the street? How do people look at you and interact with you when you exercise at the gym or while jogging? How does this differ from your life right now?

447. Have you ever been a calorie counter? Do you keep your eyes glued to the exercise machines that you use to find out exactly how many calories you have burned during your workouts? How do the "amount of calories burned" affect your exercising?

448. Have you ever had a workout and exercise buddy or group? Talk about your experiences with this group or duo and how you helped each other out? If you have never been a part of such a pair or a group, talk about working out with an ideal workout partner and how you think it might go.

449. Do you have a chronic exerciser in your life? If so, write a story about the role exercise plays in this person's day to day life. If not, create a character that uses exercise to deal with all the stress in his or her life

450. Talk about the time that you felt you were the most in shape in your entire lifetime. What things were you able to do that you aren't able to now? What would you do to get back into that kind of condition?

451. Write a story about trying to implement your ideal exercise plan as if you had unlimited resources, unlimited motivation, and no obligations throughout the day. How would you develop physically after 3 months with this plan? 6 months? A year?

452. What is the most fun you've ever had exercising? Going on a jog with someone cute? Playing a game of hoops with your friends? Detail the experience.

Creative Writing Prompts: Sleep

453. You have been tossing and turning all night and you can't seem to go to sleep. You go over to your desk and begin writing your insomniac thoughts in a stream of consciousness style. Detail that account and everything that's going on around you.

454. Talk about the first time you had to sleep in bed with someone else. Whether it is a sibling you had to share a bed with, a significant other, or just an awkward situation. How did you adjust to having someone else in there with you? If it wasn't a big deal, imagine that it was for you or the other person and run with it.

455. Discuss a recurring dream that you've had at some point in your life. Did you ever figure out the meaning? Write out all the details you can think of about the dream and then write out the possible meanings for it.

456. You have a big test the next day and you can't fall asleep because of the noises coming from the next door neighbors. Talk about your frustration, your walk over there, and the results that occur.

457. Sleep deprivation. It happened during school and it still happens in life. Talk about your attempts to survive on very little sleep and how effective they were/are.

458. Detail a day in which you've decided to stay in bed from top to bottom. You sleep on and off the entire time, waking to little interesting scenes of other people in the house with you. Talk about this crazy, lazy day.

459. What was your scariest nightmare ever? Talk about who is in it with you and why it was so frightening. Then, write an account of you going into your dream to battle the scariness of it all.

460. What is the most comfortable bed that you've ever slept on? What was it about the bed that made sleeping nearly immediate and divine? Talk about the creation of that bed as if it were some kind of magical construction.

461. The weirdest place you've ever fallen asleep: perhaps the subway, the forest, on a rooftop? Talk about your strangest sleeping location ever and what led up to it, resulted from it.

462. If you are having trouble sleeping, what is your tried and true method to make sure that you conk out? Warm milk? A little bit of TV? Go into one of

these situations in a story, and make it a sort of Mission Impossible thing to get to sleep. As if the world depended on it.

463. You no longer have to sleep. The world has been granted a full night's rest with the push of a button. What do you do with this new chunk of your day?

464. You find yourself in a lucid dream in which you can control everything. What do you change in your dream world to make it perfect?

6 FOR THE KIDS

Creative Writing Prompts: First Grade

465. You have just walked into a spooky house! What is in the spooky house? Are there any people in the house? What do they say to you?

466. What is something you love to do more than anything else in the world? Why do you like it so much?

467. What is your favorite television show? Talk about a funny scene in the show and what the characters say to each other.

468. You have found a magic wand! You can do anything with it. What do you do? Do you share the wand with anybody else?

469. Your mom and dad buy you a new big dog as a Christmas present! Talk about the dog. What does the dog do? What does he look like?

470. What do you want to be when you grow up and why? Who is the most famous person who has that job already? If you don't know, make him up!

471. Write about your teacher! What is your teacher's name, what does he or she look like, and what do you like about him or her?

472. What is your favorite food? Who makes it better your mom, dad, or a restaurant? Talk about the food and what makes it so good.

473. What do your mom and dad do for work? What do they do for fun?

474. What is your house like? What do you like the most about it? What is your favorite room in the house?

475. You have had a magic spell cast on you and you are now 30 years old! What do you do now that you don't go to school anymore? Do you get a job? Do you get married?

476. What would happen on your best possible day? Who would you see, what would you eat and what would you do?

Creative Writing Prompts: Second Grade

477. Who is your favorite famous person? What do you like about him or her and would you like to do what he or she does when you grow up? Why?

478. If you could be a character in any book or movie who would it be? What would you do differently and what would you do the same as the character? Why?

479. What is your favorite thing to do during the summer? Is it camp? Vacation? Hanging out in the house? Why do you like it so much?

480. What do you think your parents were like when they were your age? Do you think they were the same as you or different from you? Would you and your parents have been friends?

481. What is the scariest thing that's ever happened to you? Why was it so scary and how did you get away from it?

482. How big is your family? Talk a little bit about everybody from your family: brothers, sisters, grandparents, cousins, uncles. Talk about everybody!

483. What is your favorite subject in school? Do you like reading the most? Math? Science? Talk about that subject and why you like it so much.

484. Talk about a fun thing you did with your friends or family. Write about the day from the time you woke up to the time you went to sleep. What did you like so much about it?

485. What do you think is the best way to help out in your town? How could you make things better for everybody else? Write about how even one person can make a difference.

486. If you had to write a book what would it be about? Talk about some of the characters from the book and what they would be doing.

487. Your teacher has made YOU the teacher for the rest of the week. What are you going to teach the rest of the class about? How do you think they will like you?

488. Do you believe in magic and supernatural beings? Talk about some of the magical things that you believe are real in this world.

Creative Writing Prompts: Third Grade

489. What is your favorite game that you like to play? Is it something with other people or just a game that you play alone? Who would be the best people to play it with and where would you play it?

490. Talk about a time in which you felt very proud of yourself. What did you do and why did you do it? Did you receive any awards for doing this task?

491. Ten years from now what do you think the world will be like? How will things have changed and how would they change for you (you will be in your first year of college by then!)?

492. What is the best birthday party you've ever been to and why? What was the theme of the party and what did you bring as a gift (and if it was your own party, what did you get as a gift)?

493. What is your favorite movie of all time? Why is it so good? Do you remember who you were with the first time that you saw it?

494. What would you do if you were the President of the United States? How would you help people and how would you change things about the world?

495. Talk about a time that you were on a plane. What did you see when you looked out of the window? Where were you going? Do you remember if there was anything special happening on the plane itself?

496. What is the best meal that you've ever had? Who cooked it and why do you remember it so well? Do you think that you'd be able to cook the same thing if you had the chance?

497. What would you do with a million dollars? What would you buy? Would you give any of it away to charity? Which charity would you give some to?

498. What is the most memorable dream or nightmare that you've ever had? Describe the dream from the beginning to the end and try not to leave out any details.

499. If you had your choice of living anywhere in the world where would it be? Why would you live there and what do you think would change about your life?

500. What do you feel like the differences are between girls and boys in how they act? Tell a story with at least one character from each gender having a conversation.

7 LITERATURE AND GENRE

Creative Writing Prompts: Shakespeare

501. Compose a sonnet to the love of your life. This person can be living, dead, with you, not with you, etc.; it doesn't matter because it's a sonnet! Try using iambic pentameter and the rhyme schemes of the bard himself.

502. You have suddenly become transported into your favorite Shakespearian play and you are playing your favorite character. How do you interact in this new world and do you try to change your character's fate?

503. Two normal Joe's in the present day are having a regular conversation. In blank verse! Make sure to use some good iambic pentameter on this one.

504. If Shakespeare were to write a play about your life, what would it be? A comedy, a tragedy, a romance, a history, or some combination? Explain your choice and try writing the first scene (doesn't need to be in blank verse, but you might as well try :)).

505. You have stumbled on the missing link of Shakespearian evidence. You can prove if Shakespeare was in fact the writer of his own plays, if someone else wrote them, or if an entire set of different writers wrote them. Which is it, what is the evidence, and what do you do with it?

506. You are trying to convince someone to sleep with you from directly below his or her balcony. What do you say and how do you "proclaim your love?"

507. If you were to write over 30 different masterful plays, what would they be about? Write the titles of these world-changing plays, write a short description, and explain the critical reception of each of them.

508. Imagine you are part of one of those original Globe Theater audiences (in the late 16th, early 17th century). What is it like? How does it smell? Do you or any of them understand what's being said? :)

509. You have your choice of directing any Shakespearian play. The cast, set, and everything are already together, you just have to make it work. What do you choose and how do you go about it?

510. Adapt a Shakespearian plot into a story, play, or movie. It can be a loose adaptation (like the movie "10 Things I Hate About You") or something more exact. Pick one and begin to write a little bit of it (or write the entire thing).

511. Shakespeare comes over for dinner. What do you make him and what do you and your family/friends talk about with him?

512. Write a story from the perspective of one of Shakespeare's characters. The character wants to tell the world how his real life story differs from the one told in the play.

Creative Writing Prompts: Language

513. Some people say that French is the language of love. Some say it's Italian. What would be the language you would choose and why? Write a story in which a person who speaks that language comes up to you and sweeps you off your feet.

514. Talk about a time where you were especially tongue tied and it got in your way socially. You just couldn't get out the words that you wanted. If this has never happened to you, create a story in which this occurs during a particularly important social situation.

515. How important is your mastery of your primary language? Do you use it to be social, to be funny, or to be suave? What would happen if you no longer had the skill for such nuances? Write a hypothetical story in which this is the case.

516. Create a story in which you are in love with somebody who either does not speak your language or cannot speak it very well. How do you communicate and what do you try to learn from this person's language?

517. You are in a different country from your own and you only sort of speak the language there. Describe one of your days from top to bottom trying to shop, get directions, etc.

518. If you could pick 5 languages to learn, what would they be and why? How would you go about learning them and what would you do as soon as you knew them?

519. You are tutoring a student in your native language. How do you go about it and how do you explain such things as idiomatic phrases and the strange rules. Is it difficult?

520. You have a son who has just come home spouting every curse word you've ever heard in your life (and some you weren't even aware of). How do you explain to your son the context of these words and why he should use them sparingly (or not at all)?

521. Talk about an experience in which you had to use your vague experience with a language (like one you slightly learned in high school) in order to get through a situation. Perhaps you played (bad) translator to a friend at a store or in an argument? Make a situation up if you don't have one.

522. Watch a half hour of television in another language. Then write a humorous recap of the episode making wild guesses for what the characters are talking about throughout.

523. You have been forced by an evil magician to give up your language completely (can't speak it or understand when it's spoken to you) and to be given another language entirely. What do you choose?

524. Talk about a time in which you lost your voice and had to communicate without language. What did you do and how did it change the way people interacted with you?

Creative Writing Prompts: Books

525. What is your favorite (or a few of your favorites) book and why? How many times have you read it and how does it make you feel when you flip through the pages? What would you tell someone when you're recommending this book to them?

526. What is your least favorite book? Why are you so turned off by it and how would you rail against it if a friend told you he was reading it? Now imagine that you are forced to watch a movie version of the book. Describe your experience.

527. Do you remember the first book that either you read or your parents read to you? Write a story comparing the reading of this first book to you versus you reading it to your child as his or her first book.

528. A friend has recommended that you read a book that he says is "completely amazing." The book is anything but. What do you tell your friend and does this change your opinion about his taste?

529. Talk about the book that you had the hardest time getting through in school (Faulkner for me! :)). Why do you think you had such a hard time and how did you do on any subsequent tests? How did you learn enough to get by with it?

530. You have been transported into one of your favorite books as a character of your choosing. Who are you, what book is it, and what happens during your adventures? Go into extreme detail.

531. Sometimes, a friend, a parent, or a loved one just needs to take a few pieces of advice and their lives will begin to fall into place, you just know it. Take 5 people you know who need to stop being stubborn about certain things and pair each of them up with a different book. They read them and learn the lesson. What happens to them?

532. You have been given the chance to adapt a book of your choosing to the big screen! How do you go about making this book fit the typical 2 hour run time without losing any of your beloved or important elements?

533. What is your favorite place to read? Talk about why it is such a perfect spot and give a detailed account of one of your reading sessions including the book that you'd be most likely to read.

534. You are in a book club meeting! Talk about the various people that would be in a book club of yours and what book you might be reading. Even if this has never happened, make up your dream book club or the book club from hell.

535. You are writing the book of your dreams. How does it make you feel and what do you think has held you back for so long from getting it completed?

536. You are walking down the road and you come upon a group of kids burning books. What do you do next?

Creative Writing Prompts: Fantasy

537. You have stumbled upon a wand and an instruction manual. You can do pretty much anything with this magical device, but it is probably best to keep it semi-secret for the time being. Describe your first couple of weeks with this new found life hack.

538. You live in a world where cars are obsolete because griffins take everybody around (starting around 1990). How does this change traffic patterns and roads? Are you still late to school or work because of your "vehicle?"

539. The world you live in is essentially the same...present day, same technologies...except everybody lives in castles and is trying to work their way up to knighthood (including women). Detail a typical day in your life.

540. You must go on a quest to save the world from impending doom! What do you bring, who do you bring with you, and what is this evil presence that is threatening the planet?

541. You wake up in the morning and you have become a centaur. Are you the only one? How are you going to go to work or school like this? What changes have occurred in your life after this transformation?

542. You are taking your dog for a walk when he starts talking to you. In fact, all the animals in the world have just become extremely conscious and have begun talking to their masters. How does this change things? A new civil rights movement, perhaps?

543. Create your own fantasy world using any of the following elements: magic, elves, secret dungeon, a captured prince, and a self-replenishing bag of gold.

544. You have suddenly been inserted as one of the characters in the Lord of the Rings series. Who are you and do you change anything about how your character acted in the books or movies?

545. During a tornado, your house flies away "Wizard of Oz" style and ends up in a fantastical realm. Where is it and how do you go about your quest to get home?

546. You can pick a significant other from any fantasy book or movie. Who is this person and how are they in a relationship?

547. A fantasy author or filmmaker of your choice has given you 100% creative control in continuing the story (or doing a prequel). What do you do with this power?

548. Change one major element of the current world today like how people speak, how money is exchanged or how we entertain ourselves and make it something fantastical. How does this change the world?

Creative Writing Prompts: Mystery

549. You wake up to find a post-it note attached to your forehead. This note is a clue that leads you to another clue somewhere in your house. Your roommates claim ignorance but decide that they'll help you to solve the mystery. One clue continues to lead to another, where will it end?

550. There has been a murder and you are the top rated private eye in town. A mysterious woman who asks you to help with the case may also be the primary suspect. What is the evidence and how do you solve the case?

551. On a day that started like any other, your friends and family have started to treat you a bit strangely and you suspect that something is up. On a whim, you stay out a bit later then curfew. When you return your house is surrounded by police cars. What do you do?

552. You are the only eyewitness to a crime that even you don't truly understand. Both as witness protection and as an aid to the case, you team up with a special agent from the FBI. What was it you saw and how do you help to solve the crime together.

553. Someone has been stealing away the puppies from your town at night. You and a crack team of investigators (concerned people from the neighborhood and your friends) have decided to figure out the crime when the police couldn't. What do you do and how do you solve it?

554. Someone in your family's household has been stealing the cookies from the cookie jar at night. You set up an elaborate surveillance system in order to nab the culprit. Talk about you plan from beginning to end. Do you catch the thief?

555. Talk about a mystery that has occurred in your life. Start the story a bit before the event and go through the future consequences. Was the mystery ever solved?

556. Have you ever been accused of a crime that you didn't commit (small or large)? Talk about the situation from both your side and the side of the lawmakers (who may be your parents or friends). What actually happened in the situation?

557. You have been transported into a world where everything plays out like film-noir. The world is black and white and there are many asides to the camera (or voiceovers depending on your medium). Talk about a day in the life of the mystery prone noir.

558. You are out camping in the forest and you wake to find your lucky hat missing. You and your friends must track down the perpetrator, whether man or animal. Use the clues of the forest (tracking, etc.) to find this wonderful head covering.

559. You have been magically transported into the board game (or movie) Clue! How do you determine who the murderer is? Might it be you yourself?

560. You find a mysterious story left for you on your bed when you come home from work. Tell a story about how you find out the author of this strange text.

Creative Writing Prompts: Action

561. The mob has taken down your lover and imprisoned your family. Now it's time to get even! Discuss your infiltration of the mob's secret fortress and how you end up victorious against all odds?

562. Talk about a time in your life in which you were in a sort of action and adventure story. Did you have to show incredible athletic prowess or wits? Were there any big explosions? Go into extreme detail.

563. You are on the run from the police after being wrongfully accused for murder. Your only way of avoiding life in prison is to clear your name by finding the person who did this. What happens, how do you go about it, and how do you avoid capture?

564. You are a police officer involved in a high speed car chase. Go into extreme detail including all of the cars that get into accidents during your chase and how you attempt to catch the bad guys. Are you successful?

565. The bad guy almost always loses. Put yourself in the role of a bad guy during a big adventurous heist. You seem to have gotten away but from all of your movie watching you know that there is still a final act left to come. How do you avoid being just another bad guy statistic and losing?

566. After a big explosion, you need to help rescue multiple people out of a burning building. Describe the experience from explosion onward. Are you successful?

567. In one of the biggest movie action scenes of all time, James Cameron gave us a feel of what it might be like on the Titanic after its iceberg crash. Imagine that you are one of the passengers and you must avoid the many trials and tribulations of a sinking ship.

568. Imagine that you are the title character in any of the James Bond films. Go through your experiences of avoiding and causing explosions, getting in one-on-one battles, and wining and dining beautiful vixens. A day in the life

or a week in the life of this hero may give you enough material for a long while.

569. In a strange turn of events, you have found out that both of your parents are secret spies and that you have been thrown right into the middle of it. What does the reveal explain and how are you able to get out of a sticky situation that your parents have gotten into?

570. You are a hot-shot fighter pilot looking to take down an enemy battalion. How do you and your team go about it and do you emerge victorious? Go into extreme detail and look up plane information if you need to.

571. You have been hired to re-write an awful action flick. What is the movie and what do you do to it to make it not end up in the bargain bin within a few short years.

572. Today is a day like any other...except it was directed by Michael Bay! This famous Hollywood director is infamous for throwing as many explosions into a movie as possible. Write your day in the life directed by this arson auteur.

Creative Writing Prompts: Horror

573. There is a glass scratching sound on your house's windows and you get up out of bed to check it out. You look toward the windows and don't see anything. All of the sudden the glass breaks and something jumps in! What is it and what do you do next?

574. You are a high-schooler in between classes. You open up your locker to find a severed head! The head has a note on it that says, "You're next!" What do you do and how do you avoid being next?

575. The zombie apocalypse has begun! Several people you know have already become zombies and now it's a game of survival. What do you do to make sure that you are one of the people left at the end of the movie?

576. You are on vacation with your friends in a strange place. One night, one of your friends disappears and you have a strange suspicion that he's been

captured by something. What do you think happened and how do you get out of this situation alive?

577. You have been possessed by the devil! How do you deal with this and how do you make every effort to keep your soul possible? Feel free to go in a different direction from other possession movies.

578. If you had your choice of becoming any kind of vampire, which one would it be? A Twilight vampire, Buffy vampire, True Blood vampire, etc.? Pick one and tell your story of how you were turned and what resulted from that situation.

579. Write a story in which something extremely un-scary is terrorizing a small town. Try to be original and avoid using things that have already been in other horror or horror comedy stories. Have fun with it!

580. A friend of yours has had an ancient curse levied upon him. What do you do to help and what happens to him throughout the curse?

581. Hell has been unleashed on earth and you are the key to stopping the horrible consequences. What do you do to reverse the problem and what was the reason that this hell descended upon the planet?

582. There are several evil spirits that have taken over your house and part of your neighborhood's block. How do you appease the spirits or get rid of them?

583. What is your favorite horror movie? What do you like about it and how would you survive till the end? Go into extreme detail and feel free to include yourself in sequel ideas as well.

584. Re-write a day of your life in the style of these three horror movies: Event Horizon, Halloween and The Blair Witch Project.

Creative Writing Prompts: Science Fiction

585. It's an alien invasion! You are one of the first people to make contact with a new alien species. Are you able to communicate? How does everything go? Talk about the experience and the aftermath.

586. Your family, friends, and life might be a lot different...if they were in space! Imagine that everything you knew was transported to a traveling space ship. How would your day to day life change?

587. In a world greatly enhanced by new technologies (that are being developed every day) you have come up with a world-changing device that could change life as we know it. What is the device and why does it make such an impact?

588. During an archaeological dig, a new species of intelligent life has been found deep within our own planet. You have been chosen to lead the expedition with a crack team of special ops and scientists. What do you find in there and how do you interact with this new form of life?

589. You have been transported to another dimension! This world is similar to our own, but several key things are different. What are these key things, how did you get there, and how might you be able to get home (if you even wanted to)?

590. Several warriors from the future have come back to stop a horrible event in the past from happening. They will wait out their entire lifetimes to ensure that the problem doesn't occur. And they live in your neighborhood. How do you interact with these warriors and do you take on their request for help?

591. Strange weather patterns begin to form on the planet earth. You are a police officer working your shift when a man comes in and confesses to causing these weather problems. He also says that he's not sure if he can stop it. Do you believe the man? How do you two stop the problem if it's even possible?

592. While watching television you realize that the characters on the screen are talking to you. You step close enough and you are sucked into the TV set. You are now in the shows that you love and watch. What, however, happens when the shows end? Are you able to get back to the real world?

593. Imagine a world in which many different alien races are acquainted with each other and all of them live on a giant space station together. What is your role on this station and how does the interaction go for you?

594. Robots have become the new best pet! You, like most people, have a robot and while you aren't sure, it's possible that your particular pet has gained consciousness. You want to tell someone, but you are afraid that

something bad will happen to your robot as a result. What do you do?

595. How do you feel the world will change technologically in the next 100 years? 200 years? 10,000 years? What kind of things that we see in science fiction movies will actually come to pass? Time travel? Cloaking devices? Be specific and tell a story about each time period.

596. Pick an awful made for TV science fiction movie. Create a world in which it wins an Oscar.

Creative Writing Prompts: Romantic Comedy

597. You have been re-acquainted with a long lost love...just a few days before he or she is going to be married to a total jerk! You are set on getting back together with this person and you'll stop at nothing. What do you do to out this jerk and get back with the one you love?

598. Describe meeting your current or former significant other as if the entire situation was a romantic comedy. Filled with kooky characters and humorous situations, make your story into a very stereotypical rom-com.

599. What is your favorite romantic comedy movie and why? What would change about the movie if you were inserted into one of the main or supporting roles? Talk about these changes and go into extreme details.

600. You have been given the creative reigns of a multi-million dollar romantic comedy starring the actors of your choice. Who do you choose, what do you write, and how does the production go?

601. A love potion has begun to spread around the world, causing almost everybody to fall in love. Whether they want to or not! What would happen in such a world and would you be more likely to be wooed or wooing?

602. It is a major World War and almost everybody is called to arms. You and your significant other must be separated for many years at a time. Write a story about your communication and the crazy adventures on either side before coming back together.

603. What is your favorite television or movie couple of all time? What is it that made them such a fantastic couple? What can you learn from them in your own life and relationships?

604. Your parents have sat you and your siblings down to tell you the real, no-holds barred story of how they got together. Hold onto your hats, this is a doozy. Make up the wildest situation possible that your parents could have gotten into, mixing fact with fiction to show how they ended up together.

605. You are the parent of a teenager involved in a teen gross-out romantic comedy (a la American Pie). How do you get involved in the story and what do you do to make sure your son or daughter doesn't do anything you wouldn't do? Go into details and keep it from your perspective.

606. Turn a tragic book, comedy, or play into a romantic comedy. Mash up the details in such a way that there is an extremely happy ending that leaves everybody satisfied. You can do this with any medium; just have a good time with it.

607. Take a romantic comedy that you believe failed poorly and edit it in such a way that it could gain an Academy Award (or at least give you a few chuckles). Change everything that doesn't work and replace it with something that you believe would suit the story better.

608. Create a treatment for a romantic comedy with the most ridiculous possible male and female leads paired together in the craziest scenario you can think of.

Creative Writing Prompts: Writing

609. Describe the best piece of writing that you've ever constructed. What makes this the best in your mind? Also, write about what you think you would need to do to top it.

610. Describe the worst piece of writing that you've ever constructed. What did you learn from writing this piece?

611. Write a scene or story that is intentionally bad in every possible way.

612. Talk about a time in which someone praised your writing and how it made you feel. Describe the scene and the reactions of anybody else in the room upon hearing these words.

613. You have just won an award for your writing and you must give an acceptance speech that is worthy of your talents. Write your speech in its entirety and include an on-camera interview afterward for good measure.

614. Write a poem or a short story for the love of your life, past or present.

615. Talk about how your writing style has changed over the years. Write the same paragraph in your style from ten years ago, five years ago and from today. If you are especially young, this exercise can be extremely silly and fun :).

616. You have been given a magical pad of paper that makes everything that is written on it into reality. What do you write and what is your reasoning behind it?

617. Imagine a world in which writing was prized above athletics as a worldwide televised sport and you are one of the top competitors. Describe this world and what your "writing workout" would be.

618. How does writing fit into your life? Is it a hobby, a profession, a dream or something else? Write about this priority and if you would like to shift it at some point.

619. You have just had the burst of writing inspiration of a lifetime. You have negotiated your way out of your regular job for an entire week (with pay!) and you sit down to write. Describe your whirlwind of words, what you write about and the repercussions of your finished product.

620. Write the table of contents for your memoirs that you will be writing at the age of 80.

621. Talk about a time when a piece of writing changed you. Whether it is something you wrote or something you read, these words spoke to you and made you a different person. Describe how and why this piece made the world a different place.

622. You were digging around through some old stuff and you found some of your writing from long, long in the past. You cannot even remember writing it but it is truly amazing. Talk about what you do with it, who you show it to and what eventually happens as a result.

623. Guess the five strangest words that you include in your writing that you feel are quite unique to you. Write these words down and talk about how they made it into your standard writing vocabulary.

624. Talk about a time in which someone was overly critical of your writing and how it made you feel. What did you learn from this critique?

625. You are stuck in a room for two hours with the strongest critic of your work of all time. You have a copy of the work that he hates with a passion under your arm and he immediately lays into it. Describe those two hours.

626. A publisher has absolutely fallen in love with your writing. He says that any five books that you wish to publish are guaranteed (with a large advance). What are the five books that you choose: titles and descriptions? Talk about how you decide to write these five "dream" books.

627. Imagine that you have joined a writing group in your area. This group is full of writers from different backgrounds and skill levels. You present your most recent piece of writing to the group. How do they react and what are all of their comments?

628. The writing from your computer's hard drive was somehow sent out to all of your friends, family and acquaintances. This includes the stuff that you're afraid to share with everybody. It's out there and there's nothing you can do about it. What are some of the comments, compliments or concerns that you receive from these people?

629. You receive the beginning of a mysterious story or scene through text message and e-mail. The story is incredibly engaging but the author is untraceable. After weeks of the messages arriving, the author says to have the story published under a fake name and for you to take all of the profits. What do you do?

630. Imagine that you have been transported several centuries earlier without the use of a computer or a typewriter to write your words. How do you stay on task with an aching hand and a leaky quill? What do you write about? Describe the scene in extreme detail.

631. You are in a room with the five living writers who inspire you the most. What do you talk about?

632. You are in a room with the five deceased writers who inspire you the most (go with it). What do you talk about?

633. You live in a totalitarian state in which writing anything too provocative could get you killed. You refuse to take it safe and under a pen name, you write something that shakes the country to its very core. Describe your writing's impact and how the future of the country continues.

634. In an ancient time, you are the personal writer to the King and Queen of your country. What do they require you to write and what is your day to day life like living in the castle?

635. How do you feel that writing will change 200 years in the future? 1,000 year in the future? If you lived during that time, with your predictions holding true, how would you thrive as a writer?

636. Seemingly overnight, the world has become completely obsessed with writing! The economy is now completely focused on writing, both imports and exports. Children have scorned television and Facebook to take up writing. How does this change your life and how does the future play out in this new writing world?

637. What would your writing have to accomplish for you to consider yourself a true success? Describe that accomplishment and where you would go from there?

638. John Milton wrote the epic poem "Paradise Lost" while he was blind. Describe how you would write such a masterpiece with a major disability. Would it be a driving force of motivation or more of a supreme hindrance?

639. Many people say that they've done everything they can when it comes to becoming a full-fledged writer. Write a story about a person who has actually done everything he or she can. This may include submitting manuscripts to publishers, writing an eBook, taking course or anything else you can think of.

640. What is your favorite work of art about a writer? This can be a painting, a movie, a book, really anything at all. Write about how it impacts you as a writer.

641. What is your best quality as a writer and how did it become a part of your writing?

642. What is your worst quality as a writer and how did it become a part of your writing?

643. Name three attributes that you think would make you a much better writer if they were added to your persona. Talk about how you think you could obtain these new skills or traits.

644. Talk about three habits you have as a writer that you feel like you would be better without. How could you get rid of these or how do you think you could turn them into strengths.

645. If you had grand control over time, space and money, how would you change your life to suit your writing? Talk about a day in the life of this new writing-structured existence.

646. What is something in the world that inspires you to write? Why does it have this effect on you?

647. What is something in the world that makes you not want to write at all? What is it about this that makes you stop cold in your tracks?

648. What is the thing that you love the most about writing? Explain how it came to be this way.

649. What is an aspect of writing that you absolutely hate? Is there any way that you could make this aspect more fun and enjoyable?

650. If you could choose someone in history or someone living today to write a biography about, who would it be and why?

651. If you were teaching a child or a novice about writing, what are a few things that you would teach him or her and why?

652. If you could condense what your writing is "about" into one sentence, what would that be? Talk about why this explains your writing to a T.

653. How do you want your writing to affect people? Why? How does it affect people now?

654. Why are you a writer and describe how you came to make that decision about yourself.

655. What kind of writer would you call yourself? A poet? A journalist? Explain the type of writer you think you are and how that affects your writing.

656. If you were incapable of writing, what would be another way that you would express your creativity? Explain a day in the life of this new form of expression.

657. While dreaming you think of the most amazing novel you have ever conceived of. As you wake up, you scramble to a notebook and begin writing. What happens next?

658. Write about five characters that you would like to come to life (that you or someone else has created). Create a scene of these five characters coming together and interacting.

659. Were you ever taught something about writing that you wish you hadn't been? Something that later held you back? Go back to the day you were taught and write a scene about you being taught the opposite.

660. Pick a piece of your writing that will survive forever. What it is it and why do you think the people of the future need this?

661. Talk about a time when the use of substances affected your writing. This can be caffeine, alcohol, drugs or even just an extra large portion of pie.

662. You stumble upon a large pile of papers written by your writing enemy. You find a sheet of paper that heaps a great deal of praise on you and your writing. Talk about finding the praise and what you say to your "enemy" about it.

663. Put yourself in the shoes of a famous writer. What do you do for a day with his or her fans and fame?

664. Re-write a scene from an awful book or movie. Make it better or play up the things that made it awful.

665. Talk about a time when your emotions affected your writing. Did they affect them positively, negatively, subtly or some other way?

666. How do other people affect your writing? Talk about how a different people in your life change your writing after you interact with them.

667. Write a scene that portrays your ideal writing conditions.

668. Write a scene that portrays the conditions that make you not want to write a word.

669. Make a list of five things that you regret not having written about. Write a scene or story about one of them.

670. Write a paragraph or two that you would write to somebody who is down on their luck.

671. Imagine that you have a writing staff that takes care of all the annoying parts of writing. What do you do with the time you have set aside for writing without all of those hassles?

672. Write a piece of satire that makes fun of your own writing. This is a great way to point out some of your own flaws and learn to grow from them.

Creative Writing Prompts: Cartoons

673. What is your favorite cartoon you remember from your youth? What themes resonated with you as a child and how does it hold up today?

674. You have found yourself in the cartoon world of a popular movie or television show. How do you interact with the other characters and how does the style of animation affect you?

675. Which of the Disney princes or princesses would you be interested in starting a relationship with if they suddenly manifested into reality? What would a first date be like with that character?

676. How do you feel about the insurgence of computer-generated graphics in the world taking over for the typically hand-drawn work? Do you feel as though the heart has been sapped as technology has improved?

677. It's Saturday morning and you are given a chance to show several cartoon shows from any time in cartoon history for your children. Which shows do you choose and why?

678. In a cartoon battle, characters can pull out all of the stops, drawing weapons from seemingly nowhere and always surviving. Detail a cartoon battle between a hero and a villain to demonstrate how crazy it can get.

679. Pixar has set an extremely high bar when it comes to animated quality, but does it reach the pinnacle of classic Disney cartoons? How do they compare and which one comes out on top?

680. If you could live out the adventures of one classic cartoon character who would it be and why?

681. How would your own life differ if it were made into a cartoon? Would you be the main character? How would you take advantage of the new rules this world brings?

682. The Simpsons is one of the longest running television programs of all time. Write a scene in the style of the Simpsons with either people from your life or characters from the show.

683. You are given the opportunity to voice a cartoon character. Describe your visit to the voice studio and how your character turns out when he makes it onto the screen.

684. If you could turn any of your writings into a cartoon movie or television show which would you choose and why? Describe the adaptation process with a creative team of producers and directors.

8 ART

Creative Writing Prompts: Music

685. What is the most beautiful piece of music you've ever listened to? Talk about how each part of the song made you feel and why it has stuck with you. Also, relate a story in which you share it with someone else and try to prove to them how great it is.

686. Write a story about a character (or draw from personal experience) in which the character creates some amazing. This can be with any instrument (including a vocal one). What kind of song is it and how does the character feel about making it?

687. Describe your best concert experience of all time. What was the band, who did you go with, and why has it stuck with you as being so fantastic? Go into extreme detail and feel free to make use of band lyrics.

688. Most people have a genre of music that just does not appeal to them. What is yours and why? Create a dialogue between two characters: one who loves that genre and one (like you) who hates it.

689. You have the esteemed pleasure of watching your son, daughter, niece, or nephew at his or her very first band concert. Talk about how it went, how cute it was seeing little kids do music, and how off-key they were :).

690. You are the lead singer in a brand-new chart topping band! How does it feel to be so famous for creating art? What is it like having so many fans and having to keep the band happy when egos begin to clash?

691. If you could be proficient in any one instrument what would it be and why? What would you do if you had immense talent in creating music with this instrument?

692. Have you ever had a piece of music change your life? What specifically changed you and why? If you haven't, just create a character or a piece of music that would cause such a thing to occur.

693. It's hard not to associate certain pieces of music with certain people and times in your life. Write a "High Fidelity"-esque autobiographical piece about five songs that will forever be linked with particular people, for better or for worse.

694. As of the writing of this article, the television show "American Idol" has made thousands of people try out for a spot on the show. Create a story in which you go to audition (after practicing heavily I'm sure) and detail your experience at the tryout.

695. You have assembled an all-star team of producers and recording artists to record the best music album ever. Who do you bring together and how does it go?

696. What would your life be like without music and why?

Creative Writing Prompts: Acting

697. Talk about a time in which you had to act in front of people, whether during a class presentation, a school play you were roped into, or in an off-Broadway production. It doesn't matter what it was, what matters for this prompt is to talk about how you felt and what you think the "audience" thought of your performance.

698. What is your favorite acting performance of all time: movie, television, stage play or other? Why was this performance so moving and why has it stuck with you?

699. You are stepping up to the podium for your first Academy Award speech (you won for Best Actor or Actress)! What do you say and who do you thank? Also, how does the post-show party go?

700. What was your worst acting experience? Split pants on stage? Lines go completely out of your head? Totally off-key during a musical number? Booed into oblivion? Talk about it and for fun write a version in which everything instead went right.

701. You are in the cast of a well-received play or sketch comedy show. You have just found out that a big-time reviewer is going to be in the audience that night (and I'm not talking about Guffman! :)). How does it affect you and the rest of the cast? Does it change the way you decide to go about things?

702. You have just begun what was supposed to about a five minute scene during a packed-house show. Your scene partner has forgotten all of his lines and is just looking at you as if he is mute. What do you to salvage the scene and save the show?

703. What kind of style of acting most appeals to you? Are you an Uta Hagen fan? Stanislavski? David Mamet? Dissect a few of your experiences with all the styles you've encountered and decide on the one that's the most interesting to you.

704. Talk about a time in which you were so engrossed in the part you were acting that you were able to just let yourself run on autopilot. How did it go and what did you like or dislike about the experience?

705. Describe your experiences with your best and worst directors of all time. What could the bad one have learned from the good one and what lessons did you learn from working with either?

706. You have been cast in a pilot for CBS! Who do you tell first? How do you get the word out to the rest of your friends? What are your experiences like shooting the first episode and getting officially picked up for a full-season run?

707. Describe a time in which you needed to act like somebody else in real life. Did you have to pretend to like somebody for a job? Did you have to act like you enjoyed a friend's parents company? Go into extreme detail.

708. List five people who you feel are constantly "putting on a show" and never revealing their true personalities. Put them in a room together and describe the experience.

Creative Writing Prompts: Improv

709. Talk about a time in which you felt like you were purely improvising. You weren't thinking at all and just going for it from a completely subconscious perspective. How did that make you feel? Did your improv teammates notice? How did the audience or coach react?

710. Describe your reasons for doing improv. Do you truly feel as though it is a separate performance art or just a tool for creating other types of art? What would cause you to stop being an improviser?

711. What was your scariest improv experience? Who was involved and how did it turn out? Start the story from the beginning and go all the way through the end. Did you learn anything from this?

712. Who is the improviser, living or dead, that you respect the most in this world? Why do you feel that way and what have you learned from this person?

713. What is the best improv show you've ever seen in your life? Why was it so good and what do you remember from it?

714. What is the worst improv show you've ever seen in your life? What was so bad about it? Did you learn something from their mistakes? Did they learn something from their own mistakes?

715. Create some characters and write a play in the style of a Harold. It's Ok if it strays from the form from time to time, but try to stay as true to the feeling of the Harold as possible.

716. Write a story about a new improviser walking into class for the first time. What is scary and what is exciting about this new experience for the student? Feel free to use some of your own experiences in this account.

717. Where do you see improv taking you? Write a hypothetical story in which improv takes you as far as it possibly could. Talk about the ups and downs along the way and the things that you had to learn to get there.

718. If you could do an improv scene with anybody, who would it be? This person does not have to be a comedian. Describe every last detail of the scene and put it in the story word for word.

719. You have magically been given the skills of the perfect improviser. How does this change how you play and what will you do with this new found power?

720. How have you applied the tenets of improv comedy to your life? Talk about an experience where you were hindered or hurt by your skills.

9 SPORTS

Creative Writing Prompts: Baseball

721. You are out on the town the night that your city's team has won the World Series! You have been swept up in the crazy mob of fans and you will probably not be getting home until at least five in the morning. Describe your wild night.

722. Try to remember back to your first baseball game. The first time you saw semi-pro or professional players running about over the course of a wide expanse of grass or Astroturf. The first time you heard thousands of fans booing or cheering in unison for this game of bat and ball. Go into detail and if you can't remember something, make it up.

723. Describe a time in which you played some derivative of baseball. Whether it be the old ball and glove catch with your dad or friends or an actual full-length game. How did it go and how did it make you feel?

724. Put yourself in the shoes of a multi-million dollar superstar baseball player. Describe a typical baseball game day for you, keeping in mind your large expenses, your need to get to the field on time, the positive or negative fan response, and your trip back home.

725. Your town is all about high school baseball: they live it, breathe it, and revel in its success. You are a high school student and your best friend happens to be the star of the team. How does this friend react to this

compartmentalized superstardom? Does he change from the person you knew or does he really leave it on the field?

726. If you could be transported to any period in baseball history for a few weeks, which one would it be? Babe Ruth's Yankees? Steve Carlton's Phillies? The Cubs 1908 world championship team? Talk about your experiences in this new time and place in which baseball history is taking place.

727. What was your best experience with baseball? Why was it so positive and how has it affected your life?

728. What was your worst experience with baseball? Why was it so ridiculously negative and in what ways did it alter your outlook on the sport?

729. Describe yourself as a little boy or girl trying to catch a home run ball while surrounded by a bunch of drunken bleacher bums. Start at the at bat and go into minute detail as the ball comes your way.

730. Talk about (or make up) a time in which you went to a professional baseball game with a bunch of friends. One of those experiences in which you barely end up talking about (or watching) the game at all. Go into a lot of detail and have fun writing it.

731. You have become the owner of your favorite baseball team. How do you shake things up to keep your team winning?

732. Write a scene in which you explain baseball to someone who does not understand it at all.

Creative Writing Prompts: Wrestling

733. You have the ability to create two new WWE superstars who will battle each other at the next PPV (wrestling talk for Pay Per View). What are their names, costumes, signature moves, and what is their overall persona like? Go into detail and then describe the feud and match from start to finish.

734. Talk about being a spectator at either a professional or scholastic wrestling match. What is the crowd like and what is the general feeling in the air? You can draw on personal experience or make it up, but make sure to go into extreme detail.

735. You come in for your early morning weigh-in the day of a meet (your pre-match weigh in will be around 5 PM). You are 3 pounds over and you have no idea how it happened? Talk about your day and how you are going to lose 3 pounds before the match weigh-in, but how you'll still be strong enough to win your match.

736. You go out to the mat and shake hands with your opponent. You're not exactly sure how it happened, but the guy you're wrestling looks to be twice your size. Isn't that what weight classes are for? How do you get through the six minute match?

737. You have been given the position of a jobber in the WWE. What is a jobber? It is a wrestler who goes out there to lose to the big stars so that audience is happy. How do you deal with going in, losing, and collecting your paycheck just to lose again? Talk about a week in the life of your jobber career.

738. Somehow, you have been transported into the body of a huge muscle head in the midst of the 1980s. This muscle head is in a WWF old-school feud with none other than Hulk Hogan! What do you and Hogan talk about in the middle of your match? How does it feel to be wrestling one of the greats in the midst of his prime?

739. You go out to the mat to meet your opponent. It's a girl! While, this isn't completely unheard of, it's the first time that you've ever had to wrestle a girl. You look over and see the snickering of your friends. What happens in the match?

740. Your coach wants you to lose 20 pounds in the next two weeks so that you can wrestle at a different weight class. He hands you a rubber suit and says, "This is how we used to do it in the old days." Do you use the suit? Do you ask the coach about wrestlers who have died from them? Do you take it but work off the weight your own way?

741. You are in the big shower with a bunch of other wrestlers after a big practice. You are having your typical conversation about sports and gross guy stuff. Detail the conversation from beginning to end.

742. Your favorite wrestling super star has selected you in a contest to go out with him to a club and hang out for the entire night. How does the night go? What are all the crazy weird things he tells you about his life?

743. You have inherited your own amateur wrestling federation. What kind of wrestlers do you work with and how do you rival the huge monopolized WWE?

744. Create your dream wrestling match between two superstars who lived in different eras. Describe the match in extreme detail.

Creative Writing Prompts: Football

745. You are now the coach of the worst football team in the National Football League. You have about a year to whip into shape the sorriest bunch of athletes this side of the 2008 winless Detroit Lions. What do you do? Describe your process to keep your job and keep your team out of the division basement.

746. What is it that you love about watching football? Or conversely, what is it that you hate about watching football? Talk about all aspects of the game from the plays, to the commentary, to the advertisements.

747. Talk about a game of backyard football with a bunch of your friends. Recount a game that actually occurred or make up a game with your ideal teams and friends involved.

748. You have been dragged out to the sports bar for an all-day beer drinking, game-watching extravaganza! Talk about your experience and your various encounters with super fans throughout the day.

749. You are going to the Super Bowl! You have been granted the best seats in the house (50 yard line) and you even get to meet the players and coaches before the game. Go into extreme detail about how all of this goes for you. Do you get onto TV?

750. To keep with the Super Bowl theme, you are hosting the best Super Bowl party of all time! How do you plan the details of it, who do you invite, and how does it all go down?

751. You are a retired football player. While you've saved a little bit of money, it's certainly not enough to never work again. The only problem is that you didn't finish college and that you have few skills other than the gridiron game. What is your five year plan and how do the first few months go?

752. Alas, the new love of your life is a die-hard fan for your rival football team. You get along great, except on Sundays. How do you cope with your feud of Romeo and Juliet proportions?

753. What is your best football memory from either playing or watching the sport? Why did this memory stick with you for so long and what do you think could top it in the future? If anything!

754. You have inherited the ownership of a professional football team! As a lifelong fan, you get to choose to go after some of your favorite players in free agency. Talk about your first year with the team and how things go.

755. Imagine life as a 350 pound offense lineman in the NFL.

756. Describe a day in the life of a pair of best friends who are a punter and kicker respectively for a college football team traveling around the country.

10 THE OUTDOORS

Creative Writing Prompts: Water

757. Write about your first skinny-dipping experience? If you don't have one, make one up or create a situation that you could have been in when growing up. How do the other people react to being naked together? What are the feelings that you're experiencing?

758. Your boat has capsized about 20 miles off the coast of the ocean. Luckily, you have enough leg strength to keep yourself treading for a very long time. Describe the boat accident and your journey to safety over the next couple of days.

759. Try to remember back to you earliest swimming memory? Were you wearing floaties? Did you have a fun time with friends? Be specific and get into a lot of detail. If you can't remember a detail, make it up and make it interesting.

760. When you first begin to have an attraction to the opposite sex, you can't help but find swimsuits extremely flattering. Who was your first swimsuit crush and why? If anything resulted from this crush, write about it. If not, no reason not to have a little bit of fantasy in your penmanship :).

761. Imagine you have suddenly been transported into the body of the calorie-guzzling, gold-medal-winning body of Michael Phelps. How do you cope with this newfound athletic machinery? Can you win more gold medals in the next Olympics? Do you even like swimming?

762. Write about your most memorable heavy rainstorm. Were you alone or with friends? Were you outside caught in it or were you in a car or house watching the rain splash down? Be specific and go into great detail about the rain itself and how it affected the world around it.

763. What would you do if all of your possessions were ruined in a hurricane and flood? Elaborate about all that was lost and how you are going to have to live your new life.

764. Write about the most fun you've ever had at a water park or on a water ride. If you haven't been to one, make up the most elaborate water slide ever and detail your journey through it.

765. Describe in extreme detail a shower or bath. Talk about your process through it and make some connection between the cleansing and your life. For example, you could be washing the feeling of working a 9 to 5 job away with the shower. Feel free to make up some subtext for it.

766. You are in high school and throwing the best pool party ever! Go through the planning of it all the way through the exciting water filled excitement.

767. Imagine you are a goldfish trapped in a little fish bowl. How do you get through the boredom of everyday life?

768. Write a scene with your favorite anthropomorphic water animals having a conversation about their lives.

Creative Writing Prompts: Nature

769. Describe the most intimate experience you've ever had with nature. Try to remember a time in which you were truly affected by the natural world and it became a major part of who you are. If that's never happened, make it up.

770. One day, all plant life and animals just plain started to talk to you. They talk to a few other people too, so it's not like you're crazy. What do they tell you and what do you do about it?

771. You wake up one day as a frog on a lily pad. What do you do and how do you get back to your human form? Is this a Disney fairy tale or a Grimm's fairy tale? :)

772. What is your personal plan to preserve nature in your community? Even if you only spend 5 minutes a day each week, what is it you plan to do with that time? Do you even want to preserve nature?

773. Talk about a big hike or nature trail walk that you've been on. If you never have, make it up. Who were you with, what did you bring, and why do you remember it so well?

774. If you had a choice of any natural landscape to live on the planet and money was not an issue, where would you live? What would your first year there be like?

775. What is your favorite season and why? What memories have occurred during that season for you? Go into extreme detail on what you like about that season and mention what it is you don't like about the other ones.

776. Your favorite natural area is about to be changed into a shopping mall (I know, the plot of like every movie). What do you do to stop it and how do you get the community on your side?

777. In a horror-movie typesetting, nature fights back (and I'm not talking about the M. Night Shyamalan movie "The Happening"). You are stuck in the middle of a forest at night. How do you get out of this predicament and back into civilization?

778. For some reason, as if you were a Disney princess, animals of the forest begin to come out of nowhere to help you through your life. What do you do with this newfound power?

779. You can grow the garden of your choice without money or time as a hindrance. What do you grow and why? How do you keep out the rabbits? :)

780. Describe an experience in which you and ten friends all begin climbing an ancient and amazing looking tree.

Creative Writing Prompts: Animals

781. Talk about a time in which it really felt like you were using your animal instincts. This could be a time where you really felt your body and emotions took over. It could be positive or negative. Be very specific about how it felt and how you reacted afterward.

782. I know, I know, this is a little kindergarten, but if you could be any animal, what would you be and why? Detail a typical day in the life of this new animal version of you.

783. In George Orwell's book "Animal Farm," a hierarchy of animals was formed in a sort of allegory of government. If you were creating a more positive and happy hierarchy, what would it be?

784. What is your opinion on the mistreatment of animals in some slaughterhouses and chicken farms? Do you feel it is your personal responsibility to help these animals or do you feel as though the efficiency of the process is in the name of human progress? Be very specific and detailed.

785. If any mythical creature could be actually alive (unicorn, Sasquatch, ewok) which one would it be and why? Then, create a story of your discovery of this animal and how to peacefully bring it to the world's attention.

786. Who was/is your favorite childhood pet and why? Talk about some of your experiences with this pet and why you'll always keep him or her in your memory.

787. Who was/is your least favorite childhood pet and why? What are some of the things that turned you off of this pet? Do you blame the pet? The breeders? The owners?

788. You have become a bird! Pretty sweet, huh? How does the world look to you now that you can fly through the air at great speed? What are the things you have to worry about now that you no longer have bills to pay ;)?

789. If you could have any animal as a pet (that you have not previously had in your life) what would it be and why? Talk about some of your adventures with this pet and see how he or she adjusts to your current lifestyle.

790. You have become a zookeeper! You take care of pretty much everything in the zoo from the penguins to the elephants. What is it like being on the other side of the cage (assuming that you aren't already a zookeeper)? Talk about one of your typical days.

791. In a bit straight out of "The Island of Dr. Moreau" you are creating new animals by adding different parts from different animals together. What kind of crazy combinations have you created? How are you dealing with the consequences of bringing something semi-unnatural into the world?

792. Imagine life as part of a culture that truly values animals and requires them directly for various parts of your life (like the Native Americans and buffalos). How is your life different and what is a typical day like for you?

Creative Writing Prompts: Camping

793. You have just gotten out from school for the year and it's time to go to camp. What friends are you looking forward to seeing? What activities will you do?

794. It's the annual "Dad takes us camping" trip. Is this an event you look forward to or not? If you never had such a trip, imagine it, and write about how it'd go.

795. It's the biggest camping danger cliché ever: A bear! What do you do to avoid getting mauled?

796. What is the best campfire ghost story you've ever heard? If you've never heard one, make one up!

797. It is the middle of the night and you are a counselor for a camp of about 30 kids. The kids' tent collapses in the middle of the night. What happens and how do you deal with it?

798. What is your favorite camping activity? Fishing, games, campfires, nature? Create a story in which you and your best friends are doing said activity.

799. If you could camp anywhere in the world, where would it be and why? Go into extreme detail.

800. You are out camping with a grown up and he falls ill. You must lead the two of you back to safety. What do you do?

801. The crackling campfire can be so peaceful. Talk about sitting around one with your best friends.

802. You and your friends come upon an old cabin in the woods. What do you do?

803. You are a cowboy out in the Wild West in the 1800's. Describe your typical camping experience.

804. While camping in the woods you stumble upon an ancient village that has never encountered civilization. Describe the following day after discovering them.

Creative Writing Prompts: Beach

805. You are standing on the edge of the sand right before your feet are hitting the water. You stare out into the ocean. Write a story about the many thoughts going through your head.

806. Write a story about a child building a sand castle and talking through the entire story of the medieval town he is creating. The king, the queen, the knights, and all the people inside are given personalities and back stories. Be as detailed as possible.

807. Imagine that you are a crab walking along on the ocean, trying to avoid all of the people while trying to get a bit of food from every passerby is a complicated job. Talk about a day in the life of Herbert J. Crab (or whatever your name is :)).

808. Talk about a sport that you've played on the beach, whether a simple game of catch or some kind of water football hybrid. Who did you play with and how did the game go? If you've never done this, make up a story about it.

809. A beautiful individual in a swimsuit comes up to you. This person asks you to rub lotion all over his or her back. You strike up a conversation. What do you guys talk about and does anything progress from there?

810. You are somehow inserted into the movie Jaws, and while swimming at Amity Island, a great white shark begins terrorizing the beach. How do you and your "movie family" react to this and does any harm come to any of you?

811. The opportunity has presented itself for you to re-enact the famous scene from the movie From Here to Eternity as you lay on the ocean with a beautiful partner kissing and letting the water wash over you. Describe the situation in great detail. Do you really keep kissing when salt water gets in your face? :)

812. What is the most beautiful beach that you've ever been to? Describe the entire scene thoroughly and explain why the beach was such a pretty sight to behold. If you have never been to an aesthetically pleasing beach, create a story in which you had.

813. Describe a late night walk on the beach with someone. What is it you talk about and what's it like hearing the waves crash on the sand and seeing the lights of the nearby building shining at you?

814. There could be no beach without the nearby boardwalk! What is your favorite boardwalk experience, whether it is the shops and restaurants you went to, the money you spent playing skeeball, or hitting on attractive people? Go into detail and if you don't have such an experience, make it up!

815. What would be your perfect beach day? Describe the weather and the people you would be going with? Who would you see there and what activities would be occurring during your perfect stay?

816. Imagine your favorite beach 50 years ago before it had endured as much wear, tear and trash. Describe the scene as you make your way into the ocean.

11 THE MODERN WORLD

Creative Writing Prompts: Technology

817. Talk about one technology that you feel as though you could never live without. Is it television? Text messaging? The game Pong? Detail your obsession with this technology and write about a week in which it is taken away from you.

818. Imagine that television, movies, etc. were never invented. How would your family have spent the evening time when you were growing up? Do you feel as though this would have changed your family dynamic at all?

819. What if you created the next new important technology? What would it be and how would it change the world? Be creative here, don't just make up something that would be a two-day fad and then pass. I'm talking about the next iPod here people :).

820. PC or Mac and why? This is a simple prompt, but so many people are extremely passionate about this choice, I figured it might even yield more writing than some of the others. Have fun with this one. For an extra bonus, have it as a conversation between the PC guy and the Mac guy from the television commercials.

821. How would your life have been different if you'd grown up 20 years earlier? 10 years earlier? 10 years later? 20 years later? How would technology have affected your life differently? Would you be a different person today (other than age-wise)?

822. This is your rant space. Take the time to rant about a new or old technology that has inconvenienced you in some way or that you feel has a negative impact on society. Go to town!

823. Your sci-fi prompt of the hour! A technologically advanced alien race has come to Earth wanted to trade information. What new technological advances do we pick up from them and do we use them for good and evil? How does the diplomacy go with these aliens?

824. How do you feel as though technology has changed your relationships with other people? Do you consider your interpersonal connection better or worse with the innovations of texting, Twitter, Facebook, and the like? Be specific and cite several examples.

825. Talk about a time in your life where technology most helped you. It can be medically-related, socially-related; really any time that technology affected you in a positive way.

826. Talk about a time in your life where technology most hurt you. This story can involve any time that technology in any form got in your way of something, slowed you down, or literally hurt you. Be very specific.

827. You have been transported back to the middle ages with a couple of types of technology (a la "Army of Darkness" with Bruce Campbell). How do you survive and how do you get back to the present day?

828. Describe a week at a meditation camp in which technology is not allowed for an entire week.

Creative Writing Prompts: Internet

829. What is your favorite website and why? Talk about how much time you spend on it per week and the ways in which it fulfills you. What would happen if it was taken away from you?

830. Remember the days of dial-up connections? What would have happened if the world had never progressed beyond 56k modems? Detail a hypothetical story in which this is the case. What sites and phenomenon would never have happened?

831. Describe a time in which you got something for free off of the Internet that probably wasn't intentionally given away by the person who created it. Was it a Bit Torrent? An unofficially leaked trailer for a movie? Now talk about the person who created it walking into your living room the second that you get it up on your screen.

832. You have been shrunk down to the size of a byte and you are bouncing around on the Internet! What does everything look and feel like? How do you get around and how are you going to get out of there?

833. Write a story about a person meeting a significant other over the Internet. This can be an adaptation of a true story if you or someone you know used this method. Go into full detail about it going well or poorly.

834. Talk about the weirdest place you've ever gotten Internet. A Wi-Fi cafe in a foreign country? On your iPhone while you're in a restroom? Describe the situation and talk about what a person would have thought about that phenomenon only 20 years ago.

835. Several people have talked about being pioneers of the Internet. Create a humorous story in which a rag tag bunch of nerdy programmers create the Internet and then have their ideas stolen by someone like Al Gore.

836. Describe a time where you accidentally (or purposefully) found something completely inappropriate on the Internet. Then turn it into a hypothetical story in which the worst person possible (your grandmother, your teacher, etc.) walks in on you and you have to explain the situation.

837. Do you feel as though the Internet has improved your connection with people or has it taken away from that connection? Use several examples and feel free to craft a story of online social awkwardness with it.

838. Talk about a time in which you had an Internet misunderstanding, whether it is through e-mail, instant message, Facebook, Twitter, or anywhere else. If you do not have such a time, make one up. Have fun with this one, feeling free to elaborate and exaggerate.

839. If you could run one website on the Internet (and make your fortune from it) what would it be and why? This can be an existing site or one that has not yet been created.

840. Have you ever had your information leaked on the Internet? Have you ever been Internet stalked? Talk about your experiences or make up a story in this vein.

Creative Writing Prompts: Celebrity

841. You have shot up to superstardom through the ranks of the entertainment world and now you are hounded by the paparazzi every single day. How do you and your loved ones deal with this change?

842. You aren't a celebrity, but somehow you landed a date with one! What's it like going on a first date with cameras and autograph hounds continuously interrupting you?

843. A random YouTube video you created about a very political subject has become the most popular video on the site the last month or so. People from both sides of the issue have come up to you on the street. What are their reactions and how are you using the new found fame to your advantage?

844. Who is your favorite celebrity past or present and why? If you could do any activity with this person, what would it be and why? Detail a story in which you are doing that.

845. You are in charge of a charity event and you have a major celebrity as your master of ceremonies. This MC is having some sort of problem (mentally or physically) that you need to help your celebrity with in order to make your charity event go well. Talk about your experiences.

846. What is the closest you've ever been to a celebrity (i.e. Jennifer Aniston bumped into me once) and how do you tell the story to your friends? If you don't have a situation like this, make one up.

847. With YouTube and Reality TV, it seems like people are becoming celebrities for extremely silly reasons. Write about some "celebrities" that have gone down that path and what you believe the prognosis is for those folks.

848. Pick up a copy of a tabloid. Write some stories based on the ridiculous headlines held within. Celebrity comedy gold I tells ya! :)

849. If you were rich and famous how would you use your clout for charity? How would you use it for personal gain?

850. You have become known for a catch phrase that people repeat to you ever time they see you in the streets. Talk about a day in your life and how you stand hearing the same thing over and over again.

851. You have been given the power to turn 3 celebrities into normal people and 3 normal people into celebrities. Who do you pick and how does their first week go in their new roles?

852. How do you feel like the celebrities from 50 years ago would interact with the celebrities of today? Write a scene in which at least two of them meet.

Creative Writing Prompts: The American Dream

853. You have unintentionally achieved the proverbial American Dream; you have 2 kids, a white picket fence, a nice house, and a loving spouse. Work on a sort of timeline of how your next 30-50 years turn out with this situation.

854. What does the American Dream mean to you? What do you feel is your American Dream and how do you want to end up living?

855. Is the American Dream still about living comfortably with a family or is it now about living in extreme wealth and getting to do pretty much whatever you want? Cite some examples and perhaps even a back and forth between two families.

856. What would you consider to be success in American society? What would be failure? What would have to happen for you to be willing to compromise your vision of success?

857. Currently, one of the big American Dreams is to get out of debt. What has your experience been with debt and how does it affect you, your family, and your future?

858. Create a hypothetical story in which a large world event changes the American Dream drastically for the better or the worse. Go into extreme detail and perhaps tell the story from several different perspectives.

859. How do you feel the American Dream compares to the "Dream" in other countries? In comparison to them, do we set our standard too high? Too low? In the wrong place entirely? Go into detail.

860. Family is a huge part of the American Dream. How does your family compare to one of a healthy marriage, with two kids, and a dog? Where do you believe that puts you in society?

861. You have achieved the American Dream but it isn't as fulfilling as you thought it would be? How do you become satisfied with what you have or how do you end up achieving more?

862. Talk about a movie, book, or television show in which a family attempt to achieve success in America. What lessons can you learn from their journey and what things could they have done differently? Write your own story of a family attempting the same sort of thing.

863. You are granted a window into the future about 20 years. How do you and your family place in American society in that time? Have you gone up or down or stayed the same? Knowing what you know from that vision and that the future most definitely can be changed, what will you do?

864. Imagine that you are part of a family of immigrants arriving at Ellis Island with a head full of dreams. How do you and your family survive and thrive?

Creative Writing Prompts: Law

865. Write about a time in which you had a run in with the law. It may have been something as simple as being pulled over or something...a bit more serious. Talk about your experience from beginning to end and detail your emotions throughout.

866. There are many people who intentionally break certain laws because it isn't that difficult and there is very little chance that they will be caught. Do you completely follow all copyright laws and traffic laws? Talk about a time you've broken one or at least a time you've thought about breaking one.

867. Imagine that you have been accused of a crime that you didn't commit. While justice is served and you aren't convinced, talk about how the experience might change your life. Go into extreme detail.

868. If you could change one law that you think is unfair or just plain silly, what would it be and why? How would the world change for you and in general if this law was changed for the better (in your opinion)?

869. Whether it is via proxy or a person who is close to us, we almost all know someone who has been involved in an intense legal struggle, whether it is a suit, a divorce, or anything in between. Write about this person's struggles and how he or she ultimately got through it (or didn't get through it).

870. You have witnessed a crime and now you are being protected by the police to make sure that nobody comes after you. How does this change your life and what do you think this event will do for you if you are able to make your testimony?

871. You are a lawyer in a high profile case that may determine the direction our country goes in for the next 50 years. What do you believe the case might be and how do you argue for it?

872. Have you ever felt inclined (or actually gone through with) to sue someone? What was the situation and why did you or did you not go through with it? Do you think you could have won?

873. Have you ever signed a contract that you regretted? What kind of legal problems did this lead to and what ended up resulting in the situation.

874. How would you explain the legal system to a 1st grader who has to write a paper on the subject? What kind of questions does he or she ask and how do you respond to them? Go into detail and go through the time when the 1st grader gets his or her paper back.

875. Imagine that we were in a lawless state like in those post-apocalyptic movies. How would you life change and what would you do to survive such a way of living?

876. Create a scene in which a king creates five new laws that are extremely ridiculous and self-serving and how his subjects band together to change his mind.

Creative Writing Prompts: Media

877. What is the most impactful media event in your lifetime? Some who were alive when Kennedy was assassinated would list that, for example. What affected you in a big way and tell the story of how you received and reacted to that information.

878. Have you ever personally been in the media? Whether it was school-related, work-related, or just random: talk about a time that you were portrayed by the media. How did you and your friends react to this appearance?

879. You are a powerful media executive. Your company gets an exclusive story that will violate the privacy of some innocent-bystander types but it will potentially garner viewers. If you don't report it, someone else will anyway. What do you do and what do any families involved in the story have to say to you afterward?

880. World peace is upon us! In an unforeseen series of events, all war has ended and the crime rate has gone down 99%. What happens to the media after all of this? Does it go under? Does all reporting become positive? Describe a day of media coverage in this alternate world.

881. Talk about one event that you feel was overcooked by the media. Then compare it to an event that may have been under-covered. Write a hypothetical tale in which their amount of coverage is reversed. What happens?

882. Write a story about an extremely positive world event that occurred as a result of the media. What is the event and what is the lasting impact? Which news stations began this positive outcome and how did you come to personally know about it?

883. Imagine that you are a television show or movie that is desperate to get media coverage. What kind of stunt do you or your stars pull so that you can spread the awareness of your project far and wide?

884. If you could shift the balance of media coverage, changing the focus of the media to the things that you find most important, what would you change it to and why? How would a normal newscast go with this new focus?

885. Replace the newscasters that you hate the most with any celebrities or people from your life you think would be more interesting or entertaining. How would this newscast go with these new personalities?

886. You are having a conversation about politics, religion, etc. with someone who is completely controlled by the media. All of their opinions are those expressed through the media. Detail this conversation from beginning to end and do you have any success changing the mind of this person from any thoughts that you find to be ridiculous?

887. You are given the capability of promoting a giant media hoax on the scale of Orson Welles "War of the Worlds" presentation on radio. What do you spread and do you use it for the powers of good or evil? Talk about how you have made this hoax from beginning to end.

888. What are your feelings about the presence of social media like Twitter stories in the news?

Creative Writing Prompts: Nerd City

889. Talk about the nerdiest experience that you've ever had? What games were you playing and what was your topic of conversation?

890. Star Trek, Star Wars or another space adventure? Which is the best and why?

891. Create a scene about several best friends going to one of the following places: Comic-Con in San Diego, a Firefly Convention or a video game expo.

892. Joss Whedon, J.J. Abrams or someone else? Who is your favorite nerdy television and movie writer?

893. Nerdy television shows are only appreciated when they're gone! What show would you like to bring back from premature cancellation and why?

894. Which comic book hero would you want to be and why? Create a story of you saving the day.

895. Which comic book villain would you want to be and why? Create a story of you beating up a hero and some defenseless innocents.

896. You visit a shirt shop replete with ridiculously nerdy inside jokes on all of the shirts. Some examples include "All Your Bases Are Belong to Us," "Your Princess Is in Another Castle," etc. Pick your favorite ten and write a story about how people react to you on the streets.

897. You have been transported into your favorite video game. What is it and how do you get out alive?

898. Nerds tend to know and love actors and actresses that normal people have never heard of. Imagine that you and some of your non-nerdy friends run into your five favorite cult actors on the streets. What is your reaction and what do your friends say?

899. What does it mean to you to be a nerd? How has being a nerd affected you in your life both positively and negatively?

12 THE WEIRD

Creative Writing Prompts: Dark, Disturbing, and Weird

900. You wake up to find yourself in your five-year-old body and back in time. How do you spend your first 24 hours in this situation?

901. As you are walking down the street, you hear loud sirens. Before you can figure out the reason, you see a giant flash of light and you pass out. You wake up in a giant pile of rubble. What has happened and where do you go from here?

902. You go to work the morning after a long night of drinking. You notice a cheap wedding ring on your finger that wasn't there yesterday. Describe your action steps to determine what happened.

903. You answer your doorbell and you are surprised to see your grandfather standing in the doorway. Mostly because he's dead. He says, "I have some important things to tell you." Talk about your reaction and what happens next.

904. You have died. You are in hell. Discuss.

905. You have died. You are in heaven. Discuss.

906. You get a phone call from a strange number. The voice on the other line says he can reunite you with a lost love, forever. In return, he will take the life of someone close to you. He proves his power by giving you a full day with your lost love. Describe the day and your decision.

907. All of a sudden, the entire world can hear each other's thoughts. How does the planet cope?

908. After a strange encounter with a homeless person, you find yourself infused with superpowers like Superman. What do you do with your new found abilities?

909. You try a button on your new cell phone and it opens up a channel of communication between you and the Lord. What do you talk to Him/Her about?

910. While organizing your bookshelf, you notice a book called, "The Story of You." You open it to find a description of your own life up to this point. As you flip farther, it details your existence until death. What do you do?

911. Somehow, you have gained the ability of being irresistible to your preferred gender. The only problem is: you are in a monogamous long-standing relationship. Do you stay in the relationship? Do you cheat? Discuss.

912. Death gives you a choice between taking your mother or your father. Who do you choose?

913. A bank error in your favor has placed $1.2 billion dollars in your checking account. Detail the next 24 hours.

914. A car accident has left you with severe brain damage. You retain very little information and you now essentially have the capacity and vocabulary of a 2nd grader. How do you live from day to day with your condition?

915. The opportunity arises to go back in time and alter one event. What event do you alter? Describe your encounter from the past and its consequences in the present.

916. Everybody in the world has disappeared except for you. Describe your next 24 hours.

917. Something seems to have broken your emotions. Despite your best efforts, you can't seem to feel anything. How does this change your life?

918. A series of events has made you a target of the paparazzi and one of the world's most sought after celebrities. How did this happen and how are you dealing?

919. You have been given one day to live. Detail it from beginning to end.

Creative Writing Prompts: Paranormal

920. You sit up in bed and you see a ghost of one of your deceased relatives. Who is it and what is it they say to you? Does anyone else see this paranormal phenomenon?

921. Talk about an experience in which you felt an other-worldly presence. If you do not have one, make one up or talk about how a real life experience might have been influenced by some kind of ghost.

922. You have passed away and you are a ghost! There is one more thing that you have to take care of before you can get sent to the afterlife. What is it and how do you take care of it?

923. There you are, just sitting with your friends on a porch, minding your own business...and you all happen to be looking to the sky when you see what has to be a UFO. It zooms by several times and you actually get a lot of video and photos of the phenomenon. Where do you go with this evidence? Tell us the story.

924. A birthday coupon from a friend has sent you to a medium's office so that you can channel deceased people who are trying to get in contact with you. Who talks to you through the medium and do you believe him or her?

925. Strange things begin to happen in your house. Lights turn on and off. Furniture moves on its own. You may have an angry spirit in your house. What do you do to deal with this odd problem?

926. A friend calls you and tells you to come over right away. It's like a scene straight out of The Exorcist. Your friend believes that he or she has been possessed by a demon. What do you do?

927. A psychic has delivered to you a strange prophecy. Apparently, you have a destiny that you are not fulfilling by doing what you're doing. How do you determine what it is you should do with your life? Do you trust the psychic?

928. You are starting to sense things before they happen. A friend of yours tells you that you have Extra Sensory Perception (ESP). Do you believe the friend? How do you hone this ability or use it to your advantage?

929. Ho hum, it's just a random night when you begin having visions of the future. A few of the things you picture happening the next day occur exactly as you imagined them and you wonder if your long term visions will come true or not. Do you prepare for them or write everything off as coincidence?

930. What paranormal things do you believe in and what things do you think are just completely ridiculous? Write this as a dialogue between you and a friend who believes in practically everything.

931. Do you believe that people can converse with the deceased? Write a scene between yourself and a medium that apparently has this ability.

Creative Writing Prompts: Heaven and Hell

932. You have just gotten into heaven. What's it like? Is it everything you dreamed of? Who is there that you know and what do you learn now that you're in the afterlife?

933. You have just gotten into hell. Crap. What's it like? Is it everything you feared? Who is there that you know and what do you learn now that you're in the afterlife.

934. Dante was busy, so you and Virgil go walking through hell, purgatory, and heaven, seeing all of the people who ended up in each place and learning a lot of life lessons along the way. Who do you see and what does Virgil tell you?

935. Your loved one was accidentally killed and sent to hell. It's up to you to bring her back. How do you get down there and what do you tell the Devil to get her out of there?

936. Do you believe in a heaven and a hell? Why? Because my religion says so is not a complete answer, by the way. Go into extreme detail.

937. You get to Heaven and it turns out all religions were right! Right enough to get up to heaven at least. What is it like talking with members of other religions that once fought each other down on Earth?

938. You get to Hell and it turns out all religions were wrong! What is the right choice in this reality and is there any way to undo what has been done?

939. You have gotten into heaven and you get to see all of your deceased loved ones. Who are you most excited to see first? Who are you least excited to see? Go into detail.

940. You are given a choice. Go to hell for 20 years, with the ability to be re-incarnated on Earth at that time and get another choice at the end of your life. Go to heaven for eternity. What's your choice, why, and describe your first week of the choice.

941. Create a story of hell coming to Earth and heaven battling them for control of the planet. Yeah, it's a little sci-fi, but it'll at least have a lot of action. Go for it!

942. You get into heaven and G-d calls you into his office. He tells you that you have been chosen to help re-model Earth. What do you do first? Do you abuse this position at all while standing right next to the big man?

943. Talk about ten people in your life and whether you think they will go to Heaven or Hell (if you believe in it). How do you think they will fare in the afterlife?

13 GENERAL

General Creative Writing Prompts

944. Pick the person you most want to see in the world right now. Write a monologue or a letter to that person and then continue the story.

945. Write a scene between your parents (living or deceased, it doesn't matter) talking about you and your life.

946. Write down three names of important people from your past. Start writing a story or scene between three characters with those names.

947. Recount the story of your most romantic experience ever. You can change the names if you need to. Be very detailed about the entire encounter.

948. Write a story from the perspective of your favorite childhood pet. Make sure to include details about how the pet sees you and your family.

949. Write a scene about your best friends from high school talking about you while you aren't there set during the present day.

950. Go back in your mind to the moment you chose your current religious stance. Describe the feelings that occurred during your transition from a different religion or any blind following you were previously doing.

951. Go back in your mind to the moment you chose your current political stance. Describe the feelings that occurred during your transition from a different party or any blind following you were previously doing.

952. Pick a person who has betrayed you. Write a story about the moment that this occurred.

953. Try to remember the moment where you felt you lost your innocence. Write a conversation between your present self and the past version of you from that moment.

954. Write a scene about your best friends from high school talking about you while you aren't there set during your senior year of high school.

955. Write a scene or a story with the characters of your heart, your brain and your soul.

956. Pick the person you least want to see in the world right now. Write a monologue or a letter to that person and then continue the story.

957. Write about an experience that occurred outside of your current state or country that changed you in some way.

958. Dictate the most important phone call you've ever had in your life.

959. Write a scene between you and a person you betrayed, set around the time that the betrayal occurred.

960. In a sci-fi kind of style, you have magically gained the ability to change into the person you most want to be in the world, describe a day in your life.

961. Describe the last time you cried that didn't relate to a movie, television show, play or book.

962. Sit in total silence for five minutes and observe the things around you. Write a story about the sense of awareness this brings you.

963. Write a scene that reunites you with the one that got away. If it does happen to turn into a romance novel, that's perfectly fine :).

Creative Writing Prompts: Drugs

964. Talk about your most memorable experience with drugs, illegal or not, and how it affected you and the people around you. If the story is not very spicy, feel free to exaggerate to the extreme to make it more engaging for you to write.

965. Write about your experiences with the drug caffeine and how it has impacted your life and the lives of the people around you. Have you ever felt addicted or dependent on the drug? Describe a day in which it had an extreme impact.

966. Do you know of anybody who ever had a major drug problem or who passed away from a drug related issue? Write about your relationship with this person and if there is (or was) any way that you could help.

967. What (if any) illegal drugs do you feel are generally harmless and should be legalized? If you picked none, do you feel as though there are any other substances that should be made illegal?

968. You have found out that one of your neighbors is a major drug dealer. How do you deal with this knowledge and do you make any efforts to get this person in trouble?

969. You have a teenage child and you find some marijuana in his room. How do you confront the issue when you talk to him about it? How do you use your life experience as a guide?

970. You have been smoking marijuana with your buddies in your car. About five minutes later you are pulled over by the cops. What do you do?

971. Write a comedy sketch or entire screenplay based on stoner comedies like Cheech and Chong or Harold and Kumar. Feel free to make them as off the wall as you like.

972. Write a story about a character who is hard-core addicted to drugs even though he seems to be an upstanding person who leads a relatively happy life. Talk about how the character hides that part of himself and how he still manages to be a "contributing" member of society.

973. Craft a story about a rock band that is truly living the sex, drugs, and rock and roll lifestyle. How does drug use affect their music and does it impact their overall career?

974. You have the power to take away the negative effects of a particular drug and just utilize the positive effects. Which drug do you choose and how often do you use this now harmless drug?

975. Create a scene in which you have an intervention with a friend or family member to get him or her to stop using hardcore drugs.

Creative Writing Prompts: Race

976. Talk about a time in which you've dealt with racism. This can be with you being discriminated against, a friend of yours, or something you witnessed. How did it make you feel and what do you feel you should have done in that situation to improve things?

977. Have you ever felt like you were being racist? Be open and honest about this because even tiny things like a sarcastic joke or an internal opinion can be included in racism. Why do you feel as though you've formed this opinion and do you want to change it?

978. If you are black, imagine you are white, if you are white, imagine you are black, if you are neither, pick a different race from your own. Describe your new interaction with different races and how these encounters change now that you have a new color to your skin.

979. You are white and in the Deep South of the United States. You have unknowingly been invited to a Ku Klux Klan meeting. What do you do and what do you learn from the experience about this scary organization?

980. Imagine that you have a child that is dating (or considering getting married to) a member of a different race than your own. How do you deal with this? Describe at least the first meal with this person and at the most go through the entire relationship in story-form.

981. You have been asked to give a speech about racism to a group of 1st graders. What do you talk about and how do the children react?

982. Talk about a time in which you accidentally offended a person of a different race. If this has never happened, make up an instance in which it has occurred. How did you deal with your backtrack and were you able to diffuse the situation?

983. Discuss a time in which you were made uncomfortable by someone talking about race. Did you change the subject or put in your two cents? Go into great detail about what you believed the other people involved in the conversation were thinking.

984. Talk about a time in which you hung out with a friend or co-worker who was another race and noticed him or her (or yourself) experiencing judgment based on race. How did this make you feel and did you do something about it?

985. Discuss the opinions of your parents, grandparents, and previous generations on race, the terms they use for people, and the different ways that they talk about and exhibit racism.

986. Talk about a world with no racism and what it would be like.

987. How does racism impact your work place and how would it be different if no racism was present?

Creative Writing Prompts: Religion

988. Do you believe that the religion (if any) you grew up with was/is correct in its interpretation of G-d and the world? How do you reconcile the possible influence you've had from being brought up around the culture of the religion in influencing your decision?

989. Imagine a world in which your religion is one that its people are persecuted for. You are not seen as a first-class citizen as a result. How do you deal with this situation? Is there any kind of remedy for it?

990. Pick (from your religion or any really) a fun holiday full of festival and fun. Create a story of an outsider who is unfamiliar and his first experience with this holiday.

991. Talk about the most powerfully spiritual location you've ever entered. This could be a Church, a Synagogue, a giant green meadow, anywhere that you felt spiritually charged as a result of being there. Go into great depth about how this particular spirituality affected you.

992. Do you believe that people who are not of your same believe will face torment in the afterlife? If so, write about these beliefs. If not, create a character that believes this and use him or her in a dialogue or short story.

993. Talk about your spirituality. Even if you don't have a religion, talk about what makes you feel connected with something greater than yourself. If you are an atheist, this is a good time to talk about any lack of spirituality you feel in the world.

994. Write about any religious social groups you have ever been a part of during high school, college, or after. How did the people in this group have similar or different beliefs to you specifically? If you have never been part of such a group, do a bit of research and write about a character that is.

995. You fall in love and decide to get married. You and your significant other come from drastically different religious backgrounds and your family sits you down for a meal, asking you to reconcile how you will raise your children. What happens next?

996. Create a character (or use your own experience) who has converted from one religion to another religion. How did he or she come to make this decision and why? Use experiences that the character has had from both religions.

997. Have you ever been made fun of or have you ever made fun of someone else's religion? Talk about it and if there is anything that you learned from the experience.

998. You are the creator of a new religion that combines all of your philosophies and beliefs. What is it called, how does it work, and who follows you into it?

999. Talk about a time in which religion seriously affected one of your relationships.

1000. Create a world in which there is no religion whatsoever. How is society different?

ABOUT THE AUTHOR

Bryan Cohen is a writer, actor, director and producer who enjoys dabbling in both theatre and film. Bryan graduated from the University of North Carolina at Chapel Hill in 2005 with degrees in English and Dramatic Art with a minor in Creative Writing. He has written or co-written the plays *Chekhov Kegstand, Something from Nothing, Kerpow!* and *The Morning After.* He founded the website Build Creative Writing Ideas in late 2008 and he currently serves thousands of users a month. His other books include *Sharpening the Pencil: Essays on Writing, Motivation and Enjoying Your Life, 500 Writing Prompts for Kids: First Grade through Fifth Grade,* and *Writer on the Side: How to Write Your Book Around Your 9 to 5 Job.* Bryan is a full-time freelance writer and he currently lives in Chicago, Illinois.

Visit his site at build-creative-writing-ideas.com.

Made in the USA
Lexington, KY
27 December 2011